MW01235437

The Wisdom of
GEORGE ELIOT

.

The Wisdom of

GEORGE ELIOT

BORN MARY A

*Wit and Reflection From the Writings of
the Great Victorian Novelist
Marian Evans,
Known to the World As
George Eliot*

EDITED BY JERRET ENGLE

PHILOSOPHICAL
LIBRARY

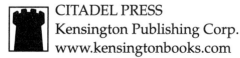

CITADEL PRESS
Kensington Publishing Corp.
www.kensingtonbooks.com

CITADEL PRESS books are published by

Kensington Publishing Corp.
850 Third Avenue
New York, NY 10022

All Kensington titles, imprints, and distributed lines are available at special quantity discounts for bulk purchases for sales promotions, premiums, fund-raising, educational, or institutional use. Special book excerpts or customized printings can also be created to fit specific needs. For details, write or phone the office of the Kensington special sales manager: Kensington Publishing Corp., 850 Third Avenue, New York, NY 10022, attn: Special Sales Department, phone 1-800-221-2647.

CITADEL PRESS is Reg. U.S. Pat. & TM Off.
The Citadel Logo is a trademark of Kensington Publishing Corp.

First printing: August 2002

10   9   8   7   6   5   4   3   2   1

Printed in the United States of America

Library of Congress Control Number: 2002100671

ISBN 0-8065-2389-1

In whatever she writes I enjoy her mind, her large,
luminous, airy mind.

—Henry James

CONTENTS

Contents

CONTENTS xi

FOREWORD

[handwritten margin notes: EVANS, BORN MARY ANN ~~EVANS~~]

The World of George Eliot

[handwritten margin notes: 1857, MARIAN, MARIAN EVANS]

In 1857, Marian Evans allowed her friend and companion George Lewes to submit stories she had written to an influential publisher he knew named John Blackwell. The stories, which she titled *Scenes of Clerical Life*, were attributed to "George Eliot," a pseudonym she had created for herself. Although she was already a published essayist and working editor, Marian was apprehensive about the project.

"... If George Eliot turns out to be a dull dog and an ineffective writer—a mere flash in the pan—I, for one, am determined to cut him on the first intimation of that disagreeable fact," she wrote.

She needn't have worried. Far from a folly, *Scenes of Clerical Life* marked the birth of one of the world's most influential fiction writers and the beginning of a literary legend.

Today, George Eliot's work is found in most modern libraries and collections—not in dusty corners, but in well-traveled spots—a dog-eared paperback or threadbare hardcover exhausted by countless readers. Why has George Eliot endured? To her fans, George Eliot is a world as much as a writer. Her staying power is the uncanny reality of her characters' inner lives. At her best, Eliot gives us characters *gentle empathy*

whose worlds may be radically different from our own, but who struggle with the same dilemmas of intellect and spirit we ourselves tangle with daily.

The quotable heart of Eliot lies in the very personal commentary she adds to her stories. While many authors use an all-knowing voice to comment on the action, Eliot's voice has a gentle empathy as well as a unique ability to take the situation so acutely observed to another level. She pinpoints common moments in all our lives and frequently adds a stunning glimmer of perspective. By the end of an Eliot novel, the reader feels a closeness and trust in this voice, like a good friend whose instincts rarely fail you.

This trust was a major reason for George Eliot's enormous popularity in the 1860s and '70s. The height of Victorian England and its soul-rattling Industrial Revolution was a period of tumultuous social change. Eliot's Victorian fans not only read her books, but wrote her countless letters, sharing their own fears and asking for sympathy and advice.

As the twentieth century got under way, Eliot's work seemed to some readers to be speaking more of a life gone by—certainly not of the infinite possibilities of that auspicious century. George Eliot fell from favor for a time. But as readers became increasingly apprehensive of the approaching Age of Technology, Eliot began to ring remarkably true once more. Writing between world wars, Virginia Woolf called Eliot's masterpiece *Middlemarch* "one of the first English novels written for grown-up people." More "grown-up" doubts about the individual's place in perilous times soon emerged. As the century progressed, George Eliot was quoted, studied by scholars, and read with enthusiasm and identification. Her popularity hit rough waters again in the turbulent 1960s and '70s, when her ardent belief in basic social values ran counter to the revolutionary tenor of those times. Individualistic to the core, Eliot had been fundamentally leery of movements, even early feminism.

But interest in Eliot rekindled as the century waned and continues as a new one begins because as we look for a moral and spiritual path through our present, some of the questions examined in Eliot's world remain uncannily contemporary. Eliot's passionate mission as arbiter between our personal journeys and society's demands and expectations continually grows more poignant. Could Marian Evans have dreamt of more for George Eliot? She would be proud.

The Real George Eliot

So who was this remarkable Marian Evans and how did she become the moral and spiritual conscience of a generation? So many generations? Her life reads like her novels: a story of great and ambitious aspirations, played out on a small, constricting stage. Like the stories of George Eliot, Marian Evans was deceptively simple and genuinely complex.

She was born Mary Anne Evans, in England, in late 1819 (she always said 1820), the youngest of a large, rather rambling family (her father had married twice). Robert Evans, her father, managed a large estate in Warwickshire for a noble family, and was well respected. His job made him something of a broker between classes. He knew and worked with the dairymen, farmers, weavers, and ribbon makers of the community as well as the aristocrats and clergy. Mr. Evans had a social fluency rare for England at that time and, as his daughter, so did young Mary Anne. While making the rounds with her father, she'd get treats from the aristocrats and their servants, and gossip from the

even the privileged led constricted lives

dairymaids and field hands. While other Victorian writers
saw an England of two major classes—the rich and poor—
Mary Anne would one day write of an England peopled
with a myriad of subtle classes and distinctions, based fundamentally on this childhood look at sociology. From her
perspective, simple spirits could envision limitless horizons
and even the privileged led constricted lives. Her beloved
father showed her the territory.

But Mary Anne and her father were on a collision course.
Mr. Evans was not an intellectual particularly and neither,
by all sketchy reports, was his second wife and Mary
Anne's mother, Christiana. Still, they sent Mary Anne to the
best local schools. These weren't much of a challenge to the
extremely bright and restless child. Under the tutelage of a
soon-beloved local teacher named Maria Lewis, eager
"Mary Ann" became devoutly Evangelical, and the *e* in her
Anne a frivolity. It was dropped. (Much comment has been
made of her habit of revising her name, seemingly to sign-
post momentous changes in her life.) Like most of the pro-
jects of Mary Ann's passionate life, she went for Evangelism
wholeheartedly. She soon forbade herself even minor fun,
as well as novels and music. She became rather a stick in the
mud about anybody else having a good time either. All of
this was undoubtedly trying at times, but conflicts over
Evangelism were not when she and her father would come
to blows.

After a few years, Mary Ann's nimble mind had pretty
much run through the major Evangelical quandaries and
begun to question its confident absolutes. It was then, when
Mary Ann was only sixteen, that her mother became ill and
died and Mary Ann's schooling was dropped so that she
could take over the household. Her father indulged her in
weekly Italian and German lessons and supported her voracious reading habit, but he expected her to run the house-

hold and care for his needs. Mary Ann's older siblings were mostly gone from home by then, and even her idolized brother Isaac was about to marry. The aging Mr. Evans had begun giving over his duties to Isaac, looking to help his son and rest on his considerable local laurels. Soon it made sense for Mary Ann and her father to give the homestead, Griff, to Isaac and his new bride and move to a smaller house in nearby Coventry. It made sense, but it was painfully lonely at first for Mary Ann. Her father became active in the local church, at least in part to help their social connections.

Coventry, however, had a silver lining. It was there Mary Ann met the Brays and the Hennells, two young, eccentric, freethinking families who loved ideas and loved to question existing notions. The Brays' home, Rosehill, had become a magnet for young liberals passing through Coventry, and even for an original-thinking foreign visitor like the American Ralph Waldo Emerson. Mary Ann's headfirst dive into friendship with the Brays and Hennells would set a pattern for relationships throughout her life: her enthusiasm for the ideas they shared manifested in a passionate, if somewhat mercurial, attachment.

Charles Hennell had written a controversial book challenging literal Biblical interpretations of Jesus' life and miracles. His book intrigued the impressionable Mary Ann and fueled her growing doubts about Evangelism. Most excitingly, her interest led to talk—dinners, debates, and letters—that challenged her extensive, if self-propelled, scholarship on the subject. Matters intensified as she also developed a crush (at the very least, depending on her biographer), on Charles Bray, Hennell's married brother-in-law. It is certain they talked often and avidly. On January 2, 1842—coincidentally while her old religious mentor, Maria Lewis, was visiting—Mary Ann reached a turning point.

She announced that, due to a profound change in her convictions, she was not going to church. And her previously patient and even indulgent father was furious.

It is so like a George Eliot novel that this date was documented and is still cited today for the earthshaking crisis it precipitated in Mary Ann's life and, in some part, in the small town of Coventry. Mary Ann came to call the crisis her declaration spurred "The Holy Wars." Essentially, her father (not actually much of a church man himself until then) was appalled. Not going to church didn't look good to the community, where he was trying to install himself, and it wasn't going to help Mary Ann find an eligible match. And that was yet another story.

Mary Ann Evans was not pretty. Her father, whom she seems to resemble from photographs, was a reasonably handsome man. Unfortunately, the same features that worked well for him were something of a disaster for Mary Ann. Pictures of Mary Ann when she had become "Marian" and was famous and flattered show a dismally uncomfortable woman with a large-featured, sensitive face, frankly unflattering hair, and insecure, complicated clothing. Nothing about Victorian fashion helped Marian, or Mary Ann before her. Her intelligence was reportedly always apparent and appealing, but Mary Ann Evans was plain and she knew it. Throughout her entire life she tried very hard to not let it bother her or determine her fate, but she was never secure enough to honestly have said it didn't matter. In the end, her intellect did triumph, but her homeliness extracted a heavy price.

At the time of the Holy Wars, her plain looks also underscored her precarious position as a twenty-one-year-old single, young lady living with her father. She was significantly without "prospects" (at least those she would consider) and dangerously close to spinsterhood. This was not the ideal position from which to launch an iconoclastic philosophical campaign. It could only irritate and tantalize the neighbors. The world did not seem to acknowledge the importance of Mary Ann's moral crisis. Most critically, her father thought it absurd. He stopped talking to Mary Ann and even seemed, at one point, to be planning to move to another, smaller home—without her. It's worth pointing out that in Victorian times, such a young lady did not strike out on her own.

The Holy War was Mary Ann's first experience with the limits of philosophical discourse, and it was to be a powerful one. Though she agonized mightily, she knew that she didn't have a lot of options. In the end, she compromised. She agreed to begin attending church with her father, even as she insisted he understand that it was an act of duty to him and not religious devotion. Her father accepted, but apparently not with appreciable gratitude, and their relationship was never the same again. Mary Ann took refuge in her friends Cara Bray and Sara Hennell to find comforting sympathy for the painful compromise. But she had marked herself in the community of Coventry as "odd" and "headstrong." On top of "plain," those labels apparently sealed her fate there, and she cared for her aging father, with only spinsterhood looming before her, until his death in 1849 when she was twenty-nine years old.

To soothe her thwarted sense of mission during this long time with her father, Mary Ann took on a project that arose through the Hennell connections, translating a controversial German work, *The Life of Christ*, by David Friedrich Strauss. Though she'd never been to Germany and only worked with her tutor at home, Mary Ann's German was very strong and she reportedly did an excellent job. It was a remarkable undertaking for an isolated young woman, and she probably would not have attempted it without the Bray and Hennell support. Eventually, (and probably through another Hennell connection) the work found a publisher, John Chapman. Publication gave the project undeniable legitimacy and helped the ambitious Mary Ann's ego enormously during the difficult years when she was wilting in her determined but underappreciated role as nursemaid and housekeeper to her failing and disappointed father.

But Mr. Evans's death did not bring an immediate release to Mary Ann; quite the contrary. Apparently still somewhat irritated by Mary Ann's behavior (and with lots of other children to endow), Evans left her only a very modest monthly allotment. She found herself with no place to live and the need to find paid work.

Outside of governess or schoolteacher (and nun or prostitute), jobs for women were scarce in Victorian England. Fond as the Brays and Hennells were of Mary Ann (and given her at times awkward devotion to both Charleses and the fact that friendship with this lonely young woman was demanding), there was apparently no opportunity offered for her to take up residence at Rosehill. Eventually her Strauss publisher John Chapman provided the answer. After several false starts, she landed in his very odd boardinghouse at 142 The Strand in London, and the new life of "Marian Evans" officially began.

With the Strauss translation as her professional credit, Mary Ann adopted the more sophisticated name "Marian" and took on the job of assistant to her publisher, John Chapman, also, incidently, the landlord of 142. Working for little more than room and board, Marian was soon indispensable to the flamboyant, if not particularly talented Chapman, and she was instrumental in making his magazine, *The Westminster Review*, a success. Chapman soon recognized this, as did his writers. But in the tradition of the time, Marian's role was uncredited, and so were the essays she began to contribute to the magazine. (Both sexes then wrote in such publications anonymously.) Still, what today would seem untenable was then a remarkable opportunity for a bright young woman.

Marian thrived in this working relationship and Chapman quickly came to value her absolutely. The problem (a recurrent one in her life) was that Marian fell in love. Chapman can't be said to have discouraged her, but he already had a jealous wife and mistress (and there were various rumors about other women boarders at 142). He did not want to risk everything for the unenticing Marian. After a brief affair she was sent ignominiously into exile, (this time she did land at Rosehill) only to be called back a few months later as Chapman discovered he really could not publish his magazine without her. The terms of their relationship were "clarified," and Marian set back to work.

The pain of all this is apparent, and it wasn't even a first for Marian. Besides her crushes on Charles Bray and Charles Hennell, she had been humiliatingly dispatched from another household she visited when her relationship with Hennell's father-in-law, one Dr. Brabant, became too intense for Mrs. Brabant's comfort. With her father gone, such disasters were made worse by the fact that Marian really had no place to go where she could heal her wounds in safety. Time after time her emotions got the better of her and she would be forced to make accommodations with the sad consequences.

These personal disasters left their marks. Although Marian was an original and almost radical thinker, her attitudes were profoundly tempered by the high prices she paid for her passions. She became increasingly sensitive to the prices others paid, too, and she never saw consequences in abstract terms. This sense of real consequences for all actions alienated her from the political or social vanguard.

What's more, she very much wanted to be liked and approved of. She never rejected society. Instead, she struggled to maintain her dignity and standards as she made a singular, if at times uneasy, peace with her reality. Her great work to come would immortalize what most of us painfully learn—that much of life is spent making accommodations, tinged at times with a little hard-earned grief.

What was exceptional about Marian Evans was that these difficult experiences didn't harden her. Her journals and letters reveal a woman who remains poignantly ready to fall in love again. That's not to say she wasn't sensitive about her trials, and perhaps that was part of the reason this particularly bruised and vulnerable "Mary Ann" character never played a major role in a George Eliot novel. Still, her vulnerabilities surely inform many themes in Eliot's work. Eliot wasn't sentimental about unrequited love: she always astutely recorded the pain.

To put her feelings for Chapman at rest, or at least channel them, Marian threw herself into her work. For four years she was the soul of *The Westminster Review*, its assistant editor and essentially editor-in-chief as well. Chapman met his role as publisher with varying degrees of ability, but he kept the enterprise afloat and enjoyed growing literary stature. Together, they published and reviewed many of the great and interesting writers of their day, from philosophers Thomas Carlyle and John Stuart Mill, to Dickens, Thackeray, Balzac, Shelley, and Charlotte Brontë. Marian herself began submitting more and more essays and joining the writers at business and social occasions. It was a thoroughly unorthodox lifestyle for a Victorian woman, but Marian flowered.

Yet, she couldn't escape the need for a special relationship to sustain her. She next grew close to Herbert Spencer, a writer and critic for *The Economist*. As its arts critic, Spencer attended theater and concerts often and Marian loved to come along. Afterward, they would debate the results, as well as science, philosophy, and world affairs, till late in the night. Spencer enjoyed her company enormously. Although Marian's relationship with Chapman remains a bit circumspect in her correspondence and journals, she left nothing ambiguous about her feelings for Spencer. She fell madly in love with him and implored him to marry her. Spencer's attitude was more complicated. At the very least he was frightened of that kind of intimacy and dismayed that Marian was not the great beauty of his dreams. He was even insensitive enough to make a point about her looks to her. (As, indeed, had Chapman.) In the end, Spencer said no categorically, but was quite happy to remain friends. Marian had no choice but to go along. It may have been Spencer's loss in the end, for he never married and to her death, jealously guarded their friendship.

But the Spencer relationship was not the complete catastrophe the others had been, for it brought Marian closer to Spencer's good friend, George Lewes. On the surface, Lewes was not a promising prospect either: he was married, he had a reputation as a lady's man and, although he doesn't look that bad in photographs, he was supposedly very ugly. A versatile writer, Lewes was somewhat unfairly seen by his London colleagues as a young man spreading himself too thin—he translated plays and wrote novels, reviews, biography, and science. Initially, Marian had little respect for his writings, though he was a regular *Westminster* contributor. Still, somehow, perhaps at first over her Spencer travails, they struck up a fast friendship. It soon became more.

Marian's friends were understandably dismayed. Lewes had a reputation as an opportunist and flirt and Marian's record with men was already disastrous. But even given Marian's reputation for impetuousness, her decision to go with Lewes to Germany (the equivalent in Victorian eyes of elopement with a married man) was a shock. The enraged talk began. The gossip shook all of literary London and sent ancillary waves of speculation across the entire city. People who had never heard of Marian or Mary Ann Evans were appropriately appalled by the conduct of this headstrong, amoral woman.

That is how British Victorian Society saw things. Marian saw something else entirely. The modern "open" marriage Lewes had with his wife, Agnes, had trapped husband and wife in a mutually unhappy relationship. While Lewes had been free to flirt and have brief affairs, Agnes had fallen in love with his friend, Thornton Hunt. Hunt was a handsome, irresponsible man who fathered four children with Agnes, on top of her four with Lewes. A man of his word, Lewes adopted all of Agnes's children, and according to Victorian law he had thereby forfeited his right of divorce, even though Agnes was willing. Now lonely and demoralized by the arrangement, Lewes wanted out of his marriage and swore he wanted to marry Marian. But there was no legal way to do so in England.

Always the moralist, Marian could never have run off with Lewes without a strong belief that this relationship was right—that it was based on mutual love and commitment. In her mind, it had to be a true marriage—that was crucial—and that was where the moral judgment lay, not in the minds of others. *"Believe no one's representations about me,"* she wrote in a heartfelt letter, *"for there is not a single person who is in a position to make a true representation."*

Though she needed to be discreet and confident in her letters, she doubtlessly agonized over this decision—and should have. For all her moral clarity, her instincts about men's abilities to love her had not served her particularly well in the past. There would be no turning back if Lewes faltered. Fortunately for her, and indeed for us, Lewes proved to be a good gamble. He seems to have been a devoted mate for twenty years, until his death in 1878. He would love her, protect her and, without exaggeration, make George Eliot possible.

For her part, Marian would fortunately always adore him. And for a considerable time, Lewes was the only person she could count on. Her family was stunned by her moving in with him. (Mary Anne had done it again.) Her brother Isaac took the action her father could not and cut her off completely, corresponding only through his solicitor and only on family business. Even her freethinking Coventry friends were distressed. Lewes's reputation on the Continent helped to make their life together there quite comfortable, but when they decided to return to England to be nearer their work and Lewes's children, it was even more difficult than they had imagined.

Conscious of and sensitive to the talk, Marian would never pay social calls again. Even at the height of her fame, the Leweses held salons at home, and Marian would make excuses not to venture into other homes or parties, fearing an uncomfortable situation. She had become an outsider. This vantage would give her considerable heartache, but also may have fueled her greatest talent.

Despite her isolation, Marian was greatly happy with Lewes from the start. With him, she willingly assumed the daunting responsibility for the many children, hustling her own writing and editing with energy to help them make ends meet. They both may have seen fiction writing in part as a moneymaker, but the path was untried enough that they deserve credit for taking the risk. Marian wrote she had dreamed of writing fiction, but scholars usually credit Lewes for helping her find the courage to undertake it. He nurtured Marian's initial attempts and willingly took on the role of her manager. As most agents discover, this role entails significant emotional support. Lewes was always there.

Marian's first endeavor, the collection of stories she entitled *Scenes of Clerical Life*, had been in her imagination a long while, she later claimed, and was directly inspired by her childhood recollections. Rather than escaping the trials of her new London life in nostalgia, however, Marian used her subject as a way to distance and focus themes that intrigued and obsessed her. Significantly for this woman whose life was tightly constricted by social realities, her interest in writing was to portray things in correspondingly unromantic terms: simple and real. The truths she had experienced in life seemed to her to need interpretation and context, perhaps, but not embroidery.

In this way she was part of a literary vanguard of her time. In the late 1800s, as the new Industrial Revolution created a class of moneyed "commoners," this middle class also became increasingly aware of the inequalities of their new, *modern* life. They saw the significant and growing gulf between the rich and poor and were less convinced than aristocrats that this was all part of God's will. To challenge the old social order, Marian, and artists like her, explored the real choices and turns of fate that separate and shape people. These were stories of commiseration and understanding, not inspiration. They were not about the gods, or kings, or nobility. They were unabashedly about us—making choices and finding a place (or not) in a changing society. The literary form we now call "realism" was just beginning. George Eliot set a standard few others would match.

Her literary ambition challenged *Scenes'* publisher, John

Blackwell, at first. He sensed the work was original and accurate and responded to the sensibility the insightful narrator in the stories shared with the reader. That voice was not pompous omniscience, but a careful, intimate self-knowledge. Still, this was new territory for popular fiction and Blackwell was in some ways brave to take it on. *Scenes* got respectful reviews and sold only modestly, but Blackwell, through Lewes, patiently encouraged "Mr. Eliot," whom he first understood to be a local clergyman.

There seems to never have been any doubt in Marian or George Lewes's minds that the George Eliot pseudonym was a necessary device. Marian was insecure enough about the fiction venture itself, and she was reluctant to further burden it with the scandal attached to her own name. Surely, she thought, if she signed her name, the work would be looked at strictly through the lens of her story—as a curiosity, not a work of art in its own right. She had her way. The book earned enough respect from Blackwell for him to encourage Lewes to send on further work from his friend, "the clergyman."

Eliot's second work, *Adam Bede,* stayed in the same world, but with more conviction and ambition. *Adam Bede* is the work that made George Eliot's reputation and forever changed Marian Evans's life. The vivid peasant characters and the illegitimate birth in its plot were unusual and considered rather scandalous by some. Yet people identified deeply with this story and the issues of love, class, and fidelity that it raised. Even Queen Victoria was a fan. Blackwell thought it strong and was eager to support it, but was probably surprised by its widespread popularity. He had lucked into a book that spoke to its times. Soon readers were clamoring to know who this George Eliot was.

Still intensely insecure, Marian was gratified by and proud of the response to *Adam Bede* but in no mind to give away her cover. Lewes himself was delighted and seems to have enjoyed his role in the deception. He was also very aware of Marian's sensitivity to criticism, and carefully filtered any even slightly critical reviews. Happily, there were many encouraging notices to share, and Marian was inspired in her third book, *Mill on the Floss,* to not only stay in her beloved Warwickshire territory, but to use many events in her own life. *Mill on the Floss* is a compendium of the pains of growing up, early love, and favorite Eliot themes like family love (and its limits) and fidelity to friends. Blackwell was delighted with it and eager to get it into print. By then he knew who George Eliot was, but was happy to help keep the secret.

This had become difficult. Marian and Lewes found themselves unable to avoid the evolving dilemma of a seedy, Warwickshire pastor named Joseph Liggins who humbly claimed to be the real George Eliot. As much as Marian wanted the protection of her pseudonym, her pride and ambition would not let someone else take credit for George Eliot. Gossip raged again. Strangers stepped forward and claimed that they were the models for characters from the books. Worst of all, there were even some insiders who whispered that Marian Evans had written the books but was too ashamed of her private life to own up. Marian wrote letters and an unsigned editorial disputing Liggins's claims, but things had gone too far. With Blackwell's somewhat reluctant encouragement, George Eliot's identity was revealed. By the time *Mill on the Floss* was published, everyone knew who George Eliot was. The book still sold well and earned praise, leaving Marian relieved and gratified. But the pseudonym was not retired.

The World and George Eliot

The secrecy surrounding George Eliot tried many of Marian's close friendships. As the ruckus died down, most of her closest friends gradually reacted with measured support. Many belatedly claimed they had guessed the truth. Some enjoyed her newfound fame, but if Marian hoped the revelation would finally bring her family's support, she was to be disappointed. Under the strict instructions of her brother Isaac, all but her sister Chrissy (whom she was helping to support financially) remained totally silent.

Still, Marian Evans was now something of a celebrity. She was sought out by male writers (like Trollope and Dickens) who were friends and came to visit. These men showed her deference and respect, but they did not bring their wives. Marian's fame would bring her only a handful of new female friends besides the few freethinking women who had stood beside Marian in friendship and in her relationship with Lewes even before she was a best-selling writer. (She would value their independence and social courage all her days.) Remarkably, the public at large proved not to be as rigid as London society. Her increasing numbers of loyal fans would continue to care less and less about the Evans/Lewes scandal. Instead, they hungrily awaited the next George Eliot novel. When even Queen Victoria's daughter asked to meet her, it seemed Marian Evans Lewes, as she now called herself, had arrived at respectability.

But Marian declined the invitation, and George Eliot remained the name on all her works. Perhaps she sensed the precarious course of celebrity could turn one way as suddenly as it had turned another. George Eliot would always be there to protect the vulnerable Marian.

Her fame and success did embolden her to try different

themes for her next few novels, and even to embark on an epic poem. These middle books were less successful than her first, but through various ups and downs, literary forms and ambitious experiments, her fans stayed loyal.

When she finally returned to her specialty—a novel about individuals and community—she was a changed woman in many ways. Her experience and social contact had greatly widened (in spite of her self-imposed exile) and her view of life was deeper—both more profound and more playful. Perhaps the distance she imposed had protected her as well from the confusion and demands of her notoriety. And she had Lewes, after all, who, in spite of having embarked on his own ambitious scientific work, liked nothing better than to keep in the middle of things. So, in spite of her isolation, *Middlemarch*, written from 1869 to 1871, is a novel acutely in touch with things—turns of phrase, personalities, politics, places—they all seem exactly right. If her public had been somewhat disappointed with her midcareer experiments, *Middlemarch* made the wait worthwhile.

Few nonautobiographical writers have lived as personally in the pages of their prose as Marian Evans. She called her novels "experiments in life." In *Middlemarch* and her next novel, *Daniel Deronda*, she perfected her point of view and trademark asides of well-wrought insight punctuated with a prick of perfectly chosen detail. The voice is wry, undeniably personal, and cuts close to the bone.

She had become a voracious observer of human nature. Even 130 years later, the characters seem to step out of our own lives. The flighty Mr. Brooke *"is a very good fellow, but pulpy; he will run into any mould, but he won't keep shape."* Mr. Vandernoodt, *from Daniel Deronda, was "an industrious gleaner of personal details and could probably tell everything about a great philosopher or physicist except his theories or dis-*

coveries." She was even secure enough to make fun of her own penchant for dispersing wisdom. In *Middlemarch*, she has Caleb Garth, not a verbal man to be sure, suddenly spout: "*the soul of a man, when it gets fairly rotten, will bear you all sorts of poisonous toad-stools, and no eye can see whence came the seed thereof.*"

Middlemarch and *Daniel Deronda* were critical and financial successes, and showcase remarkable scholarship, humor, life experience, and moral sensibility. Here is another world, yes, but a world we know with aching, personal precision. It is filled with people who embody their times and timeless aspiration—breathtakingly like people we know today—but viewed through a lens that illuminates the worn pathways between dreams and the habits of life. This is the world of George Eliot.

Two years after the publication of *Daniel Deronda*, as her own health was failing, Marion's beloved Lewes died. After a year's devastation, the ever-resilient Marian rebounded sufficiently to marry her lawyer, John Cross, a devoted young man twenty years her junior. (Upon receiving the news that she was finally in a legally recognized marriage, her long-estranged brother Isaac promptly sent a note of congratulations.) Cross was undeniably dedicated to Marian; nonetheless, he inexplicably jumped out the window into a Venetian canal on their honeymoon. (He was rescued.) Till the end, this poet of the ordinary never lived an ordinary life.

The end came suddenly, only seven months after her second marriage, when a recurrent kidney illness made a sudden, savage return. Her fans, led by the stunned but loyal Cross, rallied for the country's highest honor for her: burial in the Poets' Corner at Westminster Abbey. George Eliot's work was acknowledged to deserve it, but the lingering

aura of scandal surrounding Marian Evans Lewes empow-
ered her foes and made it impossible that she would be the
first woman so honored.

   She was buried, instead, next to George Lewes. Her novels, her wisdom, remain her monument.

Key to Abbreviations

The quotes cited in this collection are selections from George Eliot's novels, essays, and letters. Following each quotation is an abbreviation indicating its source. Further publication details may be found in the bibliography.

AB   *Adam Bede*
DD   *Daniel Deronda*
GE   *George Eliot: The Last Victorian*
FH   *Felix Holt*
MM   *Middlemarch*
MOF   *Mill on the Floss*
ROM   *Romola*
SCL   *Scenes of Clerical Life*
SM   *Silas Marner*
WR   *Westminister Review*

The Wisdom of
GEORGE ELIOT

Action

Pity that consequences are determined not by excuses but by actions!

—AB

Our deeds are like children that are born to us; they live and act apart from our own will. Nay, children may be strangled, but deeds never.

—ROM

> Deeds are the pulse of Time, his beating life,
> And righteous or unrighteous, being done,
> Must throb in after-throbs till Time itself
> Be laid in stillness, and the universe
> Quiver and breathe upon no mirror more.

—DD

Actors (Professional and Otherwise)

There are faces which nature charges with a meaning and pathos not belonging to the single human soul that flutters beneath them, but speaking the joys and sorrows of foregone generations—eyes that tell of deep love which doubtless has been and is somewhere, but not paired with those eyes—perhaps paired with pale eyes that can say nothing; just as a national language may be instinct with poetry unfelt by the lips that use it.

—AB

Advice

A full-fed fountain will be generous with its waters even in the rain, when they are worse than useless; and a fine fount of admonition is apt to be equally irrepressible.

—MM

Few friendly remarks are more annoying than the information that we are always seeming to do what we never mean to do.

—DD

Age
Old, at any rate; . . . is a gift that comes to everybody if they live long enough, so it raises no jealousy.

—DD

Ambition
High achievements demand some other unusual qualification besides an unusual desire for high prizes.

—MOF

The desire to conquer is itself a sort of subjection.

—DD

If you mean to act nobly and seek to know the best things God has put within reach of men, you must learn to fix your mind on that end, and not on what will happen to you because of it.

—ROM

Anxiety
Don't be forecasting evil, dear child, unless it is what you can guard against. Anxiety is good for nothing if we can't turn it into a defence. But there's no defence against all the things that might be.

—DD

Argument
Few things hold the perceptions more thoroughly captive
than anxiety about what we have got to say.

—MM

Art (And the Real World)
Bless us, things may be loveable that are not altogether
handsome I hope?

—AB

Paint us an angel, if you can, with a floating violet robe, . . .
paint us yet oftener a Madonna, . . . but do not impose on
us any aesthetic rules which shall banish from the region of
Art those old women scraping carrots with their work-
worn hands, . . . those rounded backs and stupid weather-
beaten faces that have bent over the spade and done the
rough work of the world . . . let us always have men ready
to give the loving pains of a life to the faithful representing
of commonplace things.

—AB

Art is the nearest thing to life; it is a mode of amplifying our
experience and extending our contact with our fellow men
beyond the bounds of our personal lot.

—Essay

It is for this rare, precious quality of truthfulness that I delight in many Dutch paintings, which lofty-minded people
despise. I find a source of delicious sympathy in these faithful pictures of a monotonous homely existence, which has
been the fate of so many more among my fellow-mortals
than a life of pomp or of absolute indigence, of tragic suffering or of world-stirring actions. I turn without shrinking
from cloud-borne angels, from prophets, sibyls, and heroic

warriors, to an old woman bending over her flower-pot, or eating her solitary dinner, while the noonday light, softened perhaps by a screen of leaves, falls on her mob-cap, and just touches the rim of her spinning-wheel, and her stone jug, and all those cheap common things which are the precious necessaries of life to her.

—AB

Bad Luck
Those who have been indulged by fortune and have always thought of calamity as what happens to others, feel a blind incredulous rage at the reversal of their lot, and half believe that their wild cries will alter the course of the storm.

—DD

Beauty
It is generally a feminine eye that first detects the moral deficiencies hidden under the "dear deceit" of beauty.

—AB

I am not at all sure that the majority of the human race have not been ugly, and even among those "lords of their kind," the British, squat figures, ill-shapen nostrils, and dingy complexions are not startling exceptions.

—AB

Human feeling is like the mighty rivers that bless the earth: it does not wait for beauty—it flows with restless force and brings beauty with it.

—AB

Beauty has an expression beyond and far above the one woman's soul that it clothes, as the words of genius have a wider meaning than the thought that prompted them: it is more than a woman's love that moves us in a woman's eyes—it seems to be a far-off mighty love that has come near to us, and made speech for itself there.

—AB

The most powerful of all beauty is that which reveals itself after sympathy and not before it. There is a charm of eye and lip which comes with every little phrase that certifies delicate perception or fine judgment, with every unostentatious word or smile that shows a heart awake to others; and no sweep of garment or turn of figure is more satisfying than that which enters as a restoration of confidence that one person is present on whom no intention will be lost.

—DD

Beginning
Men can do nothing without the make-believe of a beginning.

—DD

Being Engaged
A woman dictates before marriage in order that she may have an appetite for submission afterwards.

—MM

Being Right
Certainly, the mistakes that we male and female mortals make when we have our own way might fairly raise some wonder that we are so fond of it.

—MM

Belief
The egoism which enters into our theories does not affect their sincerity; rather, the more our egoism is satisfied, the more robust is our belief.

—MM

No one who has ever known what it is . . . to lose faith in a fellow-man whom he has profoundly loved and reverenced, will lightly say that the shock can leave the faith in the invisible goodness unshaken. With the sinking of high human trust, the dignity of life sinks too; we cease to believe in our own better self.

—ROM

Blame

It is as possible to be rigid in principle and tender in blame, as it is to suffer from the sight of things hung awry, and yet to be patient with the hanger who sees amiss.

—DD

Business

It is well known that in gambling, for example, whether of the business or holiday sort, a man who has the strength of mind to leave off when he has only ruined others, is a reformed character.

—DD

Clever persons who have nothing else to sell can often put a good price on their absence.

—DD

Challenge

Life never seems so clear and easy as when the heart is beating faster at the sight of some generous self-risking deed. We feel no doubt then what is the highest prize the soul can win; we almost believe in our own power to attain it.

—ROM

Chance

Favorable chance, I fancy, is the god of all men who follow their own devices instead of obeying a law they believe in.

—SM

Saint Anybody is a bad saint to pray to.

—DD

Character
Who can tell what just criticisms Murr the Cat may be passing on us beings of wider speculation?

—MM

Men, like planets, have both a visible and an invisible history.

—DD

Our consciousness rarely registers the beginning of a growth within us any more than without us: there have been many circulations of the sap before we detect the smallest sign of the bud.

—SM

Attempts at description are stupid: who can all at once describe a human being? even when he is presented to us we only begin that knowledge of his appearance which must be completed by innumerable impressions under differing circumstances. We recognise the alphabet; we are not sure of the language.

—DD

The touchstone by which men try us is most often their own vanity.

—ROM

A man can't very well steal a bank-note unless the bank-note lies within convenient reach; but he won't make us think him an honest man because he begins to howl at the bank-note for falling in his way.

—AB

Our deeds determine us, as much as we determine our deeds; and until we know what has been or will be the peculiar combination of outward with inward facts, which constitutes a man's critical actions, it will be better not to think ourselves wise about his character.

—AB

Ships, certainly, are liable to casualties, which sometimes make terribly evident some flaw in their construction, that would never have been discoverable in smooth water; and many a "good fellow," through a disastrous combination of circumstances, has undergone a like betrayal.

—AB

Charity
One must be poor to know the luxury of giving!

—MM

Childhood
The finest childlike faces have this consecrating power, and make us shudder anew at all the grossness and baselywrought griefs of the world, lest they should enter here and defile.

—DD

Childhood is only the beautiful and happy time in contemplation and retrospect—to the child it is full of deep sorrows, the meaning of which is unknown.

—Correspondence

Comfort
The most glutinously indefinite minds enclose some hard grains of habit; and a man has been seen lax about all his own interests except the retention of his snuff-box, concern-

The repentance which cuts off all moorings to evil, demands something more than —

ing which he was watchful, suspicious and greedy of clutch.

Selfish fear.

—MM

Compromise

The small solicitations of circumstance, . . . is a commoner history of perdition than any single momentous bargain.

—MM

Confession

The purifying influence of public confession springs from the fact, that by it the hope in lies is for ever swept away, and the soul recovers the noble attitude of simplicity.

—ROM

The repentance which cuts off all moorings to evil, demands something more than selfish fear.

—ROM

Confidence

The most obstinate beliefs that mortals entertain about themselves are such as they have no evidence for beyond a constant, spontaneous pulsing of their self-satisfaction—as it were a hidden seed of madness, a confidence that they can move the world without precise notion of a standing-place or lever.

—DD

Confidence, we know, is a comfortable disposition leading us to expect that the wisdom of providence or the folly of our friends, the mysteries of luck or the still greater mystery of our high individual value in the universe, will bring about agreeable issues, such as are consistent with our good

taste in costume, and our general preference for the best
style of thing.

—MM

Self-confidence is apt to address itself to an imaginary dulness in others; as people who are well off speak in a cajoling
tone to the poor, and those who are in the prime of life raise
their voice and talk artificially to seniors, hastily conceiving
them to be deaf and rather imbecile.

—DD

There's nothing kills a man so soon as having nobody to
find fault with but himself.

—SM

One's self-satisfaction is an untaxed kind of property which
it is very unpleasant to find depreciated.

—MM

Self-discontent which, if we know how to be candid, we
shall confess to make more than half our bitterness. . . . It always remains true that if we had been greater, circumstance
would have been less strong against us.

—MM

We hear with the more keenness what we wish others not to
hear. . . . Will not a tiny speck very close to our vision blot
out the glory of the world, and leave only a margin by
which we see the blot? I know no speck so troublesome as
self.

—MM

Conformity

Women [are] expected to have weak opinions; but the great
safeguard of society and of domestic life was that opinions

were not acted on. Sane people did what their neighbors did, so that if any lunatics were at large, one might know and avoid them.

—MM

In this stupid world most people never consider that a thing is good to be done unless it is done by their own set.

—MM

Conscience

Our mental business is carried on much in the same way as the business of State: a great deal of hard work is done by agents who are not acknowledged.

—AB

Our consciences are not all of the same pattern, an inner deliverance of fixed laws: they are the voice of sensibilities as various as our memories.

—DD

Be thankful . . . if your own soul has been spared perplexity; and judge not those to whom a harder lot has been given.

—ROM

It belongs to every large nature, when it is not under the immediate power of some strong unquestioning emotion, to suspect itself, and doubt the truth of its own impressions, conscious of possibilities beyond its own horizon.

—ROM

Conversation

One couldn't carry on life comfortably without a little blindness to the fact that everything has been said better than we can put it ourselves.

—DD

Corruption
Is it not one thing to set up a new gin-palace and another to accept an investment in an old one?

—MM

Courage
When I am frightened I find it a good thing to have somebody to be angry with for not being brave: it warms the blood.

—DD

Crabbiness
People who seem to enjoy their ill-temper have a way of keeping it in fine condition by inflicting privations on themselves.

—MOF

Crisis
There comes a terrible moment to many souls when the great movements of the world, the larger destinies of mankind, which have lain aloof in newspapers and other neglected reading, enter like an earthquake into their own lives. . . . Then it is that the submission of the soul to the Highest is tested, and even in the eyes of frivolity life looks out from the scene of human struggle with the awful face of duty, and a religion shows itself which is something else than a private consolation.

—DD

What quarrel, what harshness, what unbelief in each other can subsist in the presence of a great calamity, when all the artificial vesture of our life is gone, and we are all one with each other in primitive mortal needs?

—MOF

Criticism
When a singer has an audience of two, there is room for divided sentiments.

—MOF

The most exasperating of all criticism—that which sees vaguely a great many fine ends, and has not the least notion what it costs to reach them.

—MM

There [is] no need to praise anybody for writing a book, since it was always done by somebody else.

—MM

I think there is more than enough literature of the criticizing sort. . . . To read much of it seems to me seriously injurious: it accustoms men and women to formulate opinions instead of receiving deep impressions, and to receive deep impression is the foundation of all true mental power.

—SM

Curiosity
This wakening of a new interest—this passing from the supposition that we hold the right opinions on a subject we are careless about, to a sudden care for it, and a sense that our opinions were ignorance—is an effectual remedy for *ennui*, which unhappily cannot be secured on a physician's presciption.

—DD

Cynicism
Much of our lives is spent in marring our own influence and turning others' belief in us into a widely concluding

unbelief which they call knowledge of the world, while it is
really disappointment in you or me.

—DD

Death

Our dead are never dead to us until we have forgotten
them; they can be injured by us, they can be wounded; they
know all our penitence, all our aching sense that their place
is empty; all the kisses we bestow on the smallest relic of
their presence.

—AB

I don't know whether you strongly share, as I do, the old
belief that made men say the gods loved those who died
young. It seems to me truer than ever, now life has become
more complex and more and more difficult problems have
to be worked out. . . . to me, early death takes the aspect of
salvation—though I feel too that those who live and suffer
may sometimes have the greater blessedness of *being* a salvation.

—Correspondence

When death, the great Reconciler, has come, it is never our
tenderness that we repent of, but our severity.

—AB

Death is the only physician, the shadow of his valley the
only journeying that will cure us of age and the gathering
fatigue of years.

—Correspondence

Debt

In these days of wide commercial views and wide philosophy, according to which everything rights itself without

any trouble of ours: the fact that my tradesman is out of pocket to me, is to be looked at through the serene certainty that somebody else's tradesman is in pocket by somebody else; and since there must be bad debts in the world, why, it is mere egoism not to like that we in particular should make them instead of our fellow-citizens.

—MOF

Deserving

When events turn out so much better for a man than he has had reason to dread, is it not a proof that his conduct has been less foolish and blameworthy than it might otherwise have appeared? When we are treated well, we naturally begin to think that we are not altogether unmeritorious, and that it is only just we should treat ourselves well, and not mar our own good fortune.

—SM

Desire

When we take to wishing a great deal for ourselves, whatever we get soon turns into mere limitation and exclusion.

—DD

Desire . . . avails itself of any irrelevant scepticism, finding larger room for itself in all uncertainty about effects, in every obscurity that looks like the absence of law.

—MM

Despair

For there is no despair so absolute as that which comes with the first moments of our first great sorrow, when we have not yet known what it is to have suffered and to be healed, to have despaired and to have recovered hope.

—AB

What we call our despair is often only the painful eagerness of unfed hope.

—MM

There is something sustaining in the very agitation that accompanies the first shocks of trouble, just as an acute pain is often a stimulus, and produces an excitement which is transient strength. It is in the slow, changed life that follows—in the time when sorrow has become stale, and has no longer an emotive intensity that counteracts its pain—in the time when day follows day in dull unexpectant sameness, and trial is a dreary routine—it is then that despair threatens; it is then that the peremptory hunger of the soul is felt, and eye and ear are strained after some unlearned secret of our existence, which shall give to endurance the nature of satisfaction.

—MOF

Disappointment
We mortals, men and women, devour many a disappointment between breakfast and dinner-time; keep back the tears and look a little pale about the lips, and in answer to inquiries say, "Oh, nothing!" Pride helps us; and pride is not a bad thing when it only urges us to hide our own hurts—not to hurt others.

—MM

Discipline
Sudden impulses . . . have a false air of daemonic strength because they seem inexplicable, though perhaps their secret lies merely in the want of regulated channels for the soul to move in. . . . without which our nature easily turns to mere ooze and mud, and at any pressure yields nothing but a spurt or a puddle.

—DD

Duty

Our sense of duty must often wait for some work which shall take the place of dilettanteism [sic] and make us feel that the quality of our action is not a matter of indifference.

—MM

Duty has a trick of behaving unexpectedly—something like a heavy friend whom we have amiably asked to visit us, and who breaks his leg within our gates.

—MM

The question where the duty of obedience ends and the duty of resistance begins could in no case be an easy one.

—ROM

If the past is not to bind us, where can duty lie? We should have no law but the inclination of the moment.

—MOF

That supremely hallowed motive which men call duty . . . can have no inward constraining existence save through some form of believing love.

—ROM

We are apt to complain of the weight of duty, but when it is taken from us, and we are left at liberty to choose for ourselves, we find that the old life was the easier one.

—Correspondence

People can easily take the sacred word duty as a name for what they desire anyone else to do.

—DD

Education

It is an uneasy lot at best, to be what we call highly taught and yet not to enjoy: to be present at this great spectacle of life and never to be liberated from a small hungry shivering self—never to be fully possessed by the glory we behold, never to have our consciousness rapturously transformed into the vividness of a thought, the ardour of a passion, the energy of an action, but always to be scholarly and uninspired, ambitious and timid, scrupulous and dim-sighted.

—MM

For getting a fine flourishing growth of stupidity there is nothing like pouring out on a mind a good amount of subjects in which it feels no interest.

—MOF

Ego

Is there not a genius for feeling nobly which also reigns over human spirits and their conclusions?

—MM

They must be rather old and wise persons who are not apt to see their own anxiety or elation about themselves reflected in other minds.

—DD

The general conviction that we are admirable does not easily give way before a single negative; rather when any of Vanity's large family, male or female, find their performance received coldly, they are apt to believe that a little more of it will win over the unaccountable dissident.

—DD

It is possible to have a strong self-love without any self-satisfaction, rather with a self-discontent which is the more intense because one's own little core of egoistic sensibility is a supreme care.

—DD

Vanity is as ill at ease under indifference as tenderness is under a love which it cannot return.

—DD

It is one thing to be resolute in placing one's self out of the question, and another to endure that others should perform that exclusion for us.

—DD

Emotion
There is a great deal of unmapped country within us which would have to be taken into account in an explanation of our gusts and storms.

—DD

To have in general but little feeling, seems to be the only security against feeling too much on any particular occasion.

—MM

Men and women make sad mistakes about their own symptoms, taking their vague uneasy longings, sometimes for genius, sometimes for religion, and oftener still for a mighty love.

—MM

Empathy
Pain must enter into its glorified life of memory before it can turn into compassion.

—MM

There is no escaping the fact that want of sympathy condemns us to a corresponding stupidity.

—DD

Fly-fishers fail in preparing their bait so as to make it alluring in the right quarter, for want of a due acquaintance with the subjectivity of fishes.

—MOF

Englishmen

We English are a miscellaneous people, and any chance fifty of us will present many varieties of animal architecture or facial ornament; but it must be admitted that our prevailing expression is not that of a lively, impassioned race, preoccupied with the ideal and carrying the real as a mere makeweight. The strong point of the English gentleman pure is the easy style of his figure and clothing; he objects to marked ins and outs in his costume, and he also objects to looking inspired.

—DD

Envy

Mortals are easily tempted to pinch the life out of their neighbour's buzzing glory, and think that such killing is no murder.

—MM

Epiphanies

Looking into the eyes of death . . . passing through one of those rare moments of experience when we feel the truth of a common-place . . . is as different from what we call knowing it, as the vision of waters upon the earth is different from the delirious vision of the water which cannot be had to cool the burning tongue.

—MM

Evil

There is no sort of wrong deed of which a man can bear the punishment alone: you can't isolate yourself, and say that the evil which is in you shall not spread. Men's lives are as thoroughly blended with each other as the air they breathe: evil spreads as necessarily as disease.

—AB

Example

By being contemptible we set men's minds to the tune of contempt.

—MM

Experience

If youth is the season of hope, it is often so only in the sense that our elders are hopeful about us; for no age is so apt as youth to think its emotions, partings, and resolves are the last of their kind. Each crisis seems final, simply because it is new. We are told that the oldest inhabitants in Peru do not cease to be agitated by the earthquakes, but they probably see beyond each shock, and reflect that there are plenty more to come.

—MM

Extravagance

Expenditure—like ugliness and errors—becomes a totally new thing when we attach our own personality to it, and measure it by that wide difference which is manifest . . . between ourselves and others.

—MM

Failure

The emptiness of all things, from politics to pastimes, is never so striking to us as when we fail in them.

—DD

In all failures, the beginning is certainly the half of the whole.

—MM

Faith

Our subtlest analysis of schools and sects must miss the essential truth, unless it be lit up by the love that sees in all forms of human thought and work, the life and death struggles of separate human beings.

—SCL

A shadowy conception of power that by much persuasion can be induced to refrain from inflicting harm, is the shape most easily taken by the sense of the Invisible in the minds of men who have always been pressed close by primitive wants, and to whom a life of hard toil has never been illuminated by any enthusiastic religious faith. To them pain and mishap present a far wider range of possibilities than gladness and enjoyment.

—SM

There are many . . . souls who have absolutely needed an emphatic belief: life in this unpleasurable shape demanding some solution even to unspeculative minds; just as you inquire into the stuffing of your couch when anything galls you there, whereas eider-down and perfect French springs excite no question.

—MOF

Falling in Love

That stage of courtship which makes the most exquisite moment of youth, the freshest blossom-time of passion—when each is sure of the other's love, but no formal declaration has been made, and all is mutual divination, exalting the most trivial word, the slightest gesture, into thrills delicate and delicious as wafted jasmine scent. The explicitness of an engagement wears off this finest edge of susceptibility: it is jasmine gathered and present in a large bouquet.

—MOF

Our passions do not live apart in locked chambers, but, dressed in their small wardrobe of notions, bring their provisions to a common table and mess together, feeding out of the common store according to their appetite.

—MM

Family
The wit of a family is usually best received among strangers.

—MM

People who live at a distance are naturally less faulty than those immediately under our own eyes.

—MOF

The beings closest to us, whether in love or hate, are often virtually our interpreters of the world, and some feather-headed gentleman or lady whom in passing we regret to take as legal tender for a human being may be acting as a melancholy theory of life in the minds of those who live with them—like a piece of yellow and wavy glass that distorts form and makes colour an affliction.

—DD

Family likeness has often a deep sadness in it. Nature, that great tragic dramatist, knits us together by bone and muscle, and divides us by the subtler web of our brains; blends yearning and repulsion; and ties us by our heartstrings to the beings that jar us at every movement. We hear a voice with the very cadence of our own uttering the thoughts we despise; we see eyes—ah! so like our mother's—averted from us in cold alienation; and our last darling child startles us with the air and gestures of the sister we parted from in bitterness long years ago. The father to whom we owe our best heritage—the mechanical instinct, the keen sensibility to harmony, the unconscious skill of the modelling hand—galls us, and puts us to shame by his daily errors; the long-lost mother, whose face we begin to see in the glass as our own wrinkles come, once fretted our young souls with her anxious humours and irrational persistence.

—AB

Fate
Anyone watching keenly the stealthy convergence of human lots, sees a slow preparation of effects from one life on another, which tells like a calculated irony on the indifference or the frozen stare with which we look at our unintroduced neighbor. Destiny stands by sarcastic with our *dramatis personae* folded in her hand.

—MM

The tragedy of our lives is not created entirely from within. "Character"—says Novalis, in one of his questionable aphorisms—"character is destiny." But not the whole of our destiny. Hamlet, Prince of Denmark was speculative and irresolute, and we have a great tragedy in consequence. But if his father had lived to a good old age, and his uncle had died an early death, we can conceive Hamlet's having married Ophelia, and got through life with a reputation of sanity, notwithstanding many soliloquies, and some moody sarcasms towards the fair daughter of Polonius, to say nothing of the frankest incivility to his father-in-law.

—MOF

If it seems true that nature at certain moments seems charged with a presentment of the individual lot, must it not also be true that she seems unmindful, unconscious of another?

—AB

Fear
The idea of calling forth a show of compassion by frankly admitting an alarm or sorrow [is] necessarily intolerable [to some]. Every proud mind knows something of this experience, and perhaps it is only to be overcome by a sense of fellowship deep enough to make all efforts at isolation seem mean and petty instead of exalting.

—MM

Novelty gives immeasureableness to fear and fills the early time of all sad changes with phantoms of the future.

—DD

There is a degradation deep down below the memory that has withered into superstition.

—DD

Childhood has no forebodings; but then, it is soothed by no memories of outlived sorrow.

—MOF

First Impressions
For surely all must admit that a man may be puffed and be-lauded, envied, ridiculed, counted upon as a tool and fallen in love with, or at least selected as a future husband, and yet remain virtually unknown—known merely as a cluster of signs for his neighbours' false suppositions.

—MM

[There are] . . . those who think that nature has theatrical properties, and, with the considerate view of facilitating art and psychology, "makes up" her characters, so that there may be no mistake about them.

—AB

Friendship
The beginning of an acquaintance whether with persons or things is to get a definite outline for our ignorance.

—DD

If boys and men are to be welded together in the glow of transient feeling, they must be made of metal that will mix, else they inevitable fall asunder when the heat dies out.

—MOF

Future
It is one thing to see your road, another to cut it.

—DD

God
It is only what we are vividly conscious of that we can vividly imagine to be seen by Omniscience.

—MM

Goodness
Goodness is a large, often a prospective word; like harvest, which at one stage when we talk of it lies all underground, with an indeterminate future: is the germ prospering in the darkness? At another, it has put forth delicate green blades, and by-and-by the trembling blossoms are ready to be dashed off by an hour of rough wind or rain. Each stage has its peculiar blight, and may have the healthy life choked out of it by a particular action of the foul land

which rears or neighbours it, or by damage brought from foulness afar.

—DD

Gossip
Gossip is a sort of smoke that comes from the dirty tobacco-pipes of those who diffuse it: it proves nothing but the bad taste of the smoker.

—DD

News is often dispersed as thoughtlessly and effectively as that pollen which the bees carry off (having no idea how powdery they are) when they are buzzing in search of their particular nectar.

—MM

Human converse, I think some wise man has remarked, is not rigidly sincere.

—AB

People glorify all sorts of bravery except the bravery they might show on behalf of their nearest neighbours.

—MM

Gratitude
When gratitude has become a matter of reasoning there are many ways of escaping its bonds.

—MM

Greed
Do we not wile away moments of inanity or fatigued waiting by repeating some trivial movement or sound, until the repetition has bred a want, which is incipient habit? That will help us to understand how the love of accumulating

money grows an absorbing passion in men whose imaginations, even in the very beginning of their hoard, showed them no purpose beyond it.

—SM

When the animals entered the Ark in pairs, one may imagine that allied species made much private remark on each other, and were tempted to think that so many forms feeding on the same store of fodder were eminently superfluous, as tending to diminish the rations. (I fear the part played by the vultures on that occasion would be too painful for art to represent, those birds being disadvantageously naked about the gullet, and apparently without rites and ceremonies.)

—MM

A man who has two places, in one of which the hunting is less good, naturally [desires] a third where it is better.

—DD

Guilt

It is wonderful how much uglier things will look when we only suspect that we are blamed for them. Even our own persons in the glass are apt to change their aspect for us after we have heard some frank remark on their less admirable points.

—MM

Nemesis can seldom forge a sword for herself out of our consciences—out of the suffering we feel in the suffering we may have caused: there is rarely metal enough there to make an effective weapon.

—AB

Habit

> We please our fancy with ideal webs
> Of innovation, but our life meanwhile
> Is in the loom, where busy passion plies
> The shuttle to and fro, and gives our deeds
> The accustomed pattern.

—DD

Helplessness

The lowest depth of resignation is not to be found in martyrdom; it is only to be found when we have covered our heads in silence and felt, "I am not worthy to be a martyr; the Truth shall prosper, but not by me."

—ROM

Heritage

"No man," says a Rabbi, by way of indisputable instance, "may turn the bones of his father and mother into spoons"— sure that his hearers felt the checks against that form of economy. The market for spoons has never expanded enough for anyone to say "Why not?" and to argue that human progress lies in such an application of material. . . . The only check to be alleged is a sentiment, which will coerce none who do not hold that sentiments are the better part of the world's wealth.

—DD

[It] is perhaps a painful fact, but then, [we] know, we cannot reform our forefathers.

—AB

Heroes

Such is the irony of earthly mixtures, that the heroes have not always had carpets and teacups of their own.

—DD

We sit up at night to read about . . . Saint Francis, or Oliver Cromwell; but whether we should be glad for any one at all like them to call on us the next morning, still more, to reveal himself as a new relation, is quite another affair.

—DD

There are few prophets in the world; few sublimely beautiful women; few heroes. I can't afford to give all my love and reverence to such rarities.

—AB

Great men are over-estimated and small men are insupportable; that if you would love a woman without ever looking back on your love as a folly, she must die while you are courting her; and if you would maintain the slightest belief in human heroism, you must never make a pilgrimage to see the hero.

—AB

Hope
A man falling into dark water seeks a momentary footing even on sliding stones.

—SM

A great deal of what passes for likelihood in the world is simply the reflex of a wish.

—DD

Wishes are held to be ominous; according to which belief the order of the world is so arranged that if you have an impious objection to a squint, your offspring is the more likely to be born with one; also, that if you happen to desire a squint, you would not get it. This desponding view of probability the hopeful entirely reject, taking their wishes as good and sufficient security for all kinds of fulfillment.

—DD

The Human Experience
In each of our lives harvest and spring-time are continually one, until Death himself gathers us and sows us anew in his invisible fields.

—DD

A man . . . may head an expedition that opens new continental pathways, get himself maimed in body, and go through a whole heroic poem of resolve and endurance; and at the end of a few months he may come back to find his neighbours grumbling at the same parish grievance as before, or to see the same elderly gentleman treading the pavement in discourse with himself, shaking his head after the same percussive butcher's boy, and pausing at the same shop-window to look at the same prints.

—DD

The existence of insignificant people has very important consequences in the world. It can be shown to affect the price of bread and the rate of wages, to call forth many evil tempers from the selfish, and many heroisms from the sympathetic, and, in other ways, to play no small part in the tragedy of life.

—AB

When we are young we think our troubles a mighty business—that the world is spread out expressly as a stage for the particular drama of our lives. . . . But we begin at last to understand that these things are important only to one's own consciousness, which is but as a globule of dew on a rose-leaf that at mid-day there will be no trace of.

—Correspondence

Depend upon it, you would gain unspeakably if you would learn with me to see some of the poetry and the pathos, the tragedy and the comedy, lying in the experience of a human soul that looks out through dull grey eyes, and that speaks in a voice of quite ordinary tones.

—SCL

Human Nature

In so complex a thing as human nature we must consider it is hard to find rules without exceptions.

—AB

We are often startled by the severity of mild people on exceptional occasions; the reason is, that mild people are most liable to be under the yoke of traditional impressions.

—AB

Plotting covetousness, and deliberate contrivance, in order to compass a selfish end, are nowhere abundant but in the world of the dramatist: they demanded too intense a mental action for many of our fellow-parishioners to be guilty of them. It is easy enough to spoil the lives of our neighbours without taking so much trouble: we can do it by lazy acquiescence and lazy omission, by trivial falsities for which we hardly know a reason, by small frauds neutralised by small extravagancies, by maladroit flatteries, and clumsily improvised insinuations.

—MOF

I don't think any of the strongest effects our natures are susceptible of can ever be explained. We can neither detect the process by which they are arrived at, nor the mode in which they act on us. The greatest of painters only once painted a mysteriously divine child; he couldn't have told how he did it, and we can't tell why we feel it to be divine. I think there are stores laid up in our human nature that our understandings can make no complete inventory of.

—MOF

Human Spirit
Souls have complexions too: what will suit one will not suit another.

—MM

Humor
A difference of taste in jokes is a great strain on the affections.

—DD

Idealism
It is hard for us to live up to our own eloquence, and keep pace with our winged words, while we are treading the solid earth and are liable to heavy dining.

—DD

Ideas
After all has been said that can be said about the widening influence of ideas, it remains true that they would hardly be such strong agents unless they were taken in a solvent of feeling. The great world-struggle of developing thought is continually foreshadowed in the struggle of the affections, seeking a justification for love and hope.

—ROM

Some of the least practical ideas beat everything. They spread without being understood, and enter into the language without being thought of.

—DD

Idleness

Follows here the strict receipt
For that sauce to dainty meat,
Named Idleness, which many eat
By preference, and call it sweet:
First watch for morsels, like a hound,
Mix well with buffets, stir them round
With good thick oil of flatteries,
And froth with mean self-lauding lies.
Serve warm: the vessels you must choose
To keep it in are dead men's shoes.

—MM

Ignorance

Knowledge slowly builds up what Ignorance in an hour
pulls down.

—DD

Knowledge, through patient and frugal centuries, enlarges
discovery and makes record of it; Ignorance, wanting its
day's dinner, lights a fire with the record, and gives a
flavour to its one roast with the burnt souls of many generations.

—DD

Knowledge is power, but it is a power reined by scruple,
having a conscience of what must be and what may be;
whereas Ignorance is a blind giant who, let him but wax un-
bound, would make it a sport to seize the pillars that hold
up the long-wrought fabric of human good, and turn all the
places of joy dark as a buried Babylon.

—DD

Imagination

Imagination is a licensed trespasser: it has no fear of dogs, but may climb over walls and peep in at windows with impunity.

—AB

Immortality

One sees why it is often better for greatness to be dead, and to have got rid of the outward man.

—DD

Each of those Shining Ones had to walk on the earth among neighbours who perhaps thought much more of his gait and his garments than of anything which was to give him a title to everlasting fame: each of them had his little local personal history sprinkled with small temptations and sordid cares, which made the retarding friction of his course towards final companionship with the immortals.

—MM

Impulse

We cannot speak a loyal word and be meanly silent, we cannot kill and not kill in the same moment; but a moment is room wide enough for the loyal and mean desire, for the outlash of a murderous thought and the sharp backward stroke of repentance.

—DD

Inspiration

People who do anything finely always inspirit me to try. I don't mean that they make me believe I can do it as well. But they make the thing, whatever it may be, seem worthy to be done.

—DD

Excellence encourages one about life generally; it shows the spiritual wealth of the world.

—DD

We must learn to accommodate ourselves to the discovery that some of those cunningly-fashioned instruments called human souls have only a very limited range of music, and will not vibrate in the least under a touch that fills others with tremulous rapture or quivering agony.

—AB

Some have an emphatic belief in alcohol, and seek their *ekstasis* or outside standing-ground in gin; but the rest require something that good society calls "enthusiasm."

—MOF

Instinct
We prepare ourselves for sudden deeds by the reiterated choice of good or evil which gradually determines character.

—ROM

Jealousy
Jealousy is never satisfied with anything short of an omniscience that would detect the subtlest fold of the heart.

—MOF

There is a sort of jealousy which needs very little fire; it is hardly a passion, but a blight bred in the cloudy, damp despondency of uneasy egoism.

—MM

Jobs
Any hardship is better than pretending to do what one is paid for, and never really doing it.

—MM

Justice

So deeply inherent is it in this life of ours that men have to suffer for each other's sins, so inevitably diffusive is human suffering, that even justice makes its victims, and we can conceive no retribution that does not spread beyond its mark in pulsations of unmerited pain.

—MOF

Who shall put his finger on the work of justice and say, "It is there"? Justice is like the Kingdom of God—it is not without us as a fact, it is within us as a great yearning.

—ROM

Knowledge

It must be admitted that many well-proved facts are dark to the average man, even concerning the action of his own heart and the structure of his own retina.

—DD

Subjects are apt to appear stupid to the young as light seems dim to the old.

—DD

Ignorance gives one a large range of probabilities.

—DD

Age does not easily distinguish between what it needs to express and what youth needs to know—distance seeming to level the objects of memory.

—DD

That dead anatomy of culture which turns the universe into a mere ceaseless answer to queries, and knows not everything, but everything else about everything—as if one should be ignorant of nothing concerning the scent of violets except the scent itself for which one had no nostril.

—DD

Lame Excuses
Our firmest convictions are often dependent on subtle impressions for which words are quite too coarse a medium.

—AB

Language
A patent deodorized and non resonant language . . . effects the purpose of communication as perfectly and rapidly as algebraic signs. [Such a] language may be a perfect medium of expression to science, but will never express *life,* which is a great deal more than science.

—Essays

Leadership
A character at unity with itself—that performs what it intends, subdues every counteracting impulse, and has no visions beyond the distinctly possible—is strong by its very negations.

—MOF

Our guides, we pretend, must be sinless: as if those were not often the best teachers who only yesterday got corrected for their mistakes.

—DD

I have understood from persons versed in history, that mankind is not disposed to look narrowly into the conduct of great victors when their victory is on the right side.

—MOF

We can only have the highest happiness, such as goes along with being a great man, by having wide thoughts, and much feeling for the rest of the world as for ourselves; and this sort of happiness often brings so much pain with it, that we can only tell it from pain by its being what we would choose before everything else, because our souls see it is good. There are so many things wrong and difficult in the world, that no man can be great—he can hardly keep himself from wickedness—unless he gives up thinking much about pleasure or rewards, and gets strength to endure what is hard and painful.

—ROM

Leisure
Leisure is gone.... Ingenious philosophers tell you, perhaps, that the great work of the steam-engine is to create leisure for mankind. Do not believe them: it only creates a vacuum for eager thought to rush in. Even idleness is eager now.

—AB

Lies
Falsehood is so easy, truth so difficult.

—AB

Examine your words well, and you will find that even when you have no motive to be false, it is a very hard thing to say the exact truth, even about your own immediate feelings.

—AB

Under every guilty secret there is hidden a brood of guilty wishes.... The contaminating effect of deeds often lies less in the commission than in the consequent adjustment of our desires—the enlistment of our self-interest on the side of falsity.

—ROM

Prevarication and white lies which a mind that keeps itself ambitiously pure is as uneasy under as a great artist under the false touches that no eye detects but his own, are worn as lightly as mere trimmings when once the actions have become a lie.

—SM

We are so made, almost all of us, that the false seeming which we have thought of with painful shrinking when beforehand in our solitude it has urged itself on us as a necessity, will possess our muscles and move our lips as if nothing . . . when once we have come under the stimulus of expectant eyes and ears.

—ROM

Limits
Every limit is a beginning as well as an ending.

—AB

Little Boys
Nature has the deep cunning which hides itself under the appearance of openness, so that simple people think they can see through her quite well, and all the while she is secretly preparing a refutation of their confident prophecies. Under these average boyish physiognomies that she seems to turn off by the gross, she conceals some of her most rigid, inflexible purposes, some of her most unmodifiable characters.

—MOF

A boy's sheepishness is by no means a sign of overmastering reverence; and while you are making encouraging advances to him under the idea that he is overwhelmed by a sense of your age and wisdom, ten to one he is thinking you extremely queer.

—MOF

Loneliness

We are all islands . . . and this seclusion is sometimes the most intensely felt at the very moment your friend is caressing you or consoling you.

—Correspondence

Lost Opportunities

I suppose it is the way with all men and women who reach middle age without the clear perception that life never *can* be thoroughly joyous, under the vague dullness of the grey hours, dissatisfaction seeks a definite object, and finds it in the privation of an untried good.

—SM

Love

Perfect love has a breath of poetry which can exalt the relations of the least instructed human beings.

—SM

The subtly-varied drama between man and woman is often such as can hardly be rendered in words put together like dominoes, according to obvious fixed marks. The word of all work, Love will no more express the myriad modes of mutual attraction, than the word Thought can inform you what is passing through your neighbour's mind.

—DD

Strong love hungers to bless, and not merely to behold blessing.

—DD

Our caresses, our tender words, our still rapture under the influence of autumn sunsets, or pillared vistas, or calm majestic statues, or Beethoven symphonies . . . our emotion in its keenest moment passes from expression into silence; our love at its highest flood rushes beyond its object, and loses itself in the sense of divine mystery.

—AB

The disappointment of a youthful passion has effects as incalculable as those of smallpox, which may make one person plain and a genius, another less plain and more foolish. . . . Everything depends—not on the mere fact of disappointment, but—on the nature affected and the force that stirs it.

—DD

The vindication of the loved object is the best balm affection can find for its wounds: "A man must have so much on his mind," is the belief by which a wife often supports a cheerful face under rough answers and unfeeling words.

—SM

How could the rose help it when several bees in succession took its sweet odour as a sign of personal attachment?

—DD

The vainest woman is never thoroughly conscious of her own beauty till she is loved by the man who sets her own passion vibrating in return.

—AB

For you shall never . . . incline him who hath no love to believe that there is good ground for loving. As we may learn from the order of word-making, wherein *love* precedeth *lovable*.

—DD

People who love downy peaches are apt not to think of the stone, and sometimes jar their teeth terribly against it.

—AB

The first sense of mutual love excludes other feelings; it will have the soul all to itself.

—AB

So much of our early gladness vanishes utterly from our memory: we can never recall the joy with which we laid our heads on our mother's bosom or rode on our father's back in childhood; doubtless that joy is wrought up into our nature, as the sunlight of long-past mornings is wrought up in the soft mellowness of the apricot, but it is gone for ever from our imagination, and we can only *believe* in the joy of childhood. But the first glad moment in our first love is a vision which returns to us to the last, and brings with it a thrill of feeling intense and special as the recurrent sensation of a sweet odour breathed in a far-off hour of happiness.

—AB

It seems to me it's the same with love and happiness as with sorrow—the more we know of it the better we can feel what other people's lives are or might be.

—AB

Mankind
In many of our neighbours' lives, there is much not only of error and lapse, but of a certain exquisite goodness which can never be written or even spoken—only divined by each of us, according to the inward instruction of our own privacy.

—DD

Marriage
What greater thing is there for two human souls, than to feel that they are joined for life—to strengthen each other in all labour, to rest on each other in all sorrow, to minister to

each other in all pain, to be one with each other in silent un-speakable memories at the moment of the last parting?

—AB

When a man has seen the woman whom he would have chosen if he had intended to marry speedily, his remaining a bachelor will usually depend on her resolution rather than his.

—MM

The fact is unalterable, that a fellow-mortal with whose na-ture you are acquainted solely through the brief entrances and exits of a few imaginative weeks called courtship, may, when seen in the continuity of married companionship, be disclosed as something better or worse than what you have preconceived, but will certainly not appear altogether the same. And it would be astonishing to find how soon the change is felt if we had no kindred changes to compare it with. To share lodging with a brilliant dinner-companion, or to see your favourite politician in the Ministry, may bring about changes quite as rapid: in these cases too we begin by knowing too little and believing too much, and we some-times end by inverting the quantities.

—MM

One may be sure that whenever a marriage of any mark takes place, male acquaintances are likely to pity the bride, female acquaintances the bridegroom.

—DD

Marriage, which has been the bourne of so many narratives, is still a great beginning, as it was to Adam and Eve, who kept their honeymoon in Eden, but had their first little one among the thorns and thistles of the wilderness.

—MM

Very slight things make epochs in married life.

—ROM

Some set out, like Crusaders of old, with a glorious equipment of hope and enthusiasm, and get broken by the way, wanting patience with each other and the world.

—MM

The early months of marriage often are times of critical tumult—whether that of a shrimp-pool or of deeper waters—which afterwards subsides into cheerful peace.

—MM

There may come a moment when even an excellent husband who has dropt smoking under more or less of a pledge during courtship, for the first time will introduce his cigar-smoke between himself and his wife, with the tacit understanding that she will have to put up with it.

—DD

There are answers which, in turning away wrath, only send it to the other end of the room, and to have a discussion coolly waived when you feel that justice is all on your side is even more exasperating in marriage than in philosophy.

—MM

Marriage must be a relation either of sympathy or of conquest.

—ROM

Marriage is so unlike everything else. There is something even awful in the nearness it brings.

—MM

A Bad Marriage

The door-sill of marriage once crossed, expectation is concentrated on the present. Having once embarked on your marital voyage, it is impossible not to be aware that you make no way and that the sea is not within sight—that, in fact, you are exploring an enclosed basin.

—MM

There is no compensation for the woman who feels that the chief relation of her life has been no more than a mistake. . . . The deepest secret of human blessedness has half whispered itself to her and then forever passed her by.

—ROM

Martyrdom

Here and there is born a Saint Theresa, foundress of nothing, whose loving heartbeats and sobs after an unattained goodness tremble off and are dispersed among hindrances, instead of centering in some long-recognisable deed.

—MM

Many Theresas have been born who found for themselves no epic life wherein there was a constant unfolding of far-resonant action; perhaps only a life of mistakes, the offspring of a certain spiritual grandeur ill-matched with the meanness of opportunity; perhaps a tragic failure which found no sacred poet and sank unwept into oblivion. With dim lights and tangled circumstance they tried to shape their thought and deed in noble agreement; but after all, to common eyes their struggles seemed mere inconsistency and formlessness; for these later-born Theresas were helped by no coherent social faith and order which could perform the function of knowledge for the ardently willing soul. Their ardour alternated between a vague ideal and the common yearning of womanhood; so that the one was disapproved as extravagance, and the other condemned as a lapse.

—MM

That is the path we all like when we set out on our abandonment of egoism—the path of martyrdom and endurance, where the palm-branches grow, rather than the steep highway of tolerance, just allowance, and self-blame, where there are no leafy honours to be gathered and worn.

—MOF

There are personages who feel themselves tragic because they march into a palpable morass, dragging another with them, and then cry out against all the gods.

—DD

Memory

Memory, when duly impregnated with ascertained facts, is sometimes surprisingly fertile.

—SM

The memory has as many moods as the temper, and shifts its scenery like a diorama.

—MM

The terror of being judged sharpens memory: it sends an inevitable glare over that long-unvisited past which has been habitually recalled only in general phrases. . . .With memory set smarting like a re-opened wound, a man's past is not simply a dead history, an outworn preparation of the present: it is not a repented error shaken loose from the life: it is a still quivering part of himself, bringing shudders and bitter flavours and the tinglings of a merited shame.

—MM

The secret of our emotions never lies in the bare object but in its subtle relations to our own past: no wonder the secret escapes the unsympathising observer, who might as well put on his spectacles to discern odours.

—AB

In bed our yesterdays are too oppressive: if a man can only get up, though it be but to whistle or to smoke, he has a present which offers some resistance to the past.

—AB

Memory gets sadly diluted with time, and is not strong enough to revive us.

—AB

Our delight in the sunshine on the deep-bladed grass today, might be no more than the faint perception of wearied souls, if it were not for the sunshine and the grass in the far-off years which still live in us, and transform our perception into love.

—MOF

There's no disappointment in memory, and one's exaggerations are always on the good side.

—DD

All long-known objects, even a mere window fastening or a particular door-latch, have sounds which are a sort of recognized voice to us—a voice that will thrill and awaken, when it has been used to touch deep-lying fibres.

—MOF

Scenes of . . . earlier life [come] between . . . everything else, as obstinately as when we look through the window from a lighted room, the objects we turn our backs on are still before us, instead of the grass and trees. The successive events inward and outward were there in one view: though each might be dwelt on in turn, the rest still kept their hold in the consciousness.

—MM

Old men's eyes are like old men's memories, they are strongest for things a long way off.

—ROM

Men

[It is the] power of generalizing which gives men so much the superiority in mistake over the dumb animals.

—MM

One of the lessons a woman most rarely learns, is never to talk to an angry or a drunken man.

—AB

When a young man has a fine person, no eccentricity of manners, the education of a gentleman, and a present income, it is not customary to feel a prying curiosity about his way of thinking or his peculiar tastes. . . . Later, when he is getting rather slovenly and portly, his peculiarities are more distinctly discerned, and it is taken as a mercy if they are not highly objectionable.

—DD

The remote worship of a woman throned out of their reach plays a great part in men's lives, but in most cases the worshipper longs for some queenly recognition, some approving sign by which his soul's sovereign may cheer him without descending from her high place.

—MM

Boys are such a trouble—we could never put up with them, if we didn't make believe they were worth more.

—DD

Middle Age

In the multitude of middle-aged men who go about their vocations in a daily course determined for them much in the same way as the tie of their cravats, there is always a good number who once meant to shape their own deeds and alter the world a little. The story of their coming to be shapen after the average and fit to be packed by the gross, is hardly ever told even in their consciousness; for perhaps their ardour in generous unpaid toil cooled as imperceptibly as the ardour of other youthful loves, till one day their earlier self walked like a ghost in its old home and made the new furniture ghastly. Nothing in the world more subtle than the process of their gradual change! In the beginning they inhaled it unknowingly: you and I may have sent some of our breath towards infecting them, when we uttered our conforming falsities or drew our silly conclusions: or perhaps it came with the vibrations from a woman's glance.

—MM

It is something cruelly incomprehensible to youthful natures, this sombre sameness in middle-aged and elderly people, whose life has resulted in disappointment and discontent, to whose faces a smile becomes so strange that the sad lines all about the lips and brow seem to take no notice of it, and it hurries away again for want of a welcome. "Why will they not kindle up and be glad sometimes?" thinks young elasticity. "It would be so easy if they only liked to do it."

—MOF

The middle-aged who have lived through their strongest emotions, but are yet in the time when memory is still half passionate and not merely contemplative, should surely be a sort of natural priesthood, whom life has disciplined and consecrated to be the refuge and rescue of early stumblers and victims of self-despair.

—MOF

The Mind

So much subtler is a human mind than the outside tissues which make a sort of blazonry or clock-face for it.

—MM

Mistakes

Perhaps nothing [would] be a lesson to us if it didn't come too late. It's well we should feel . . . life's a reckoning we can't make twice over; there's no real making amends in this world, any more, nor can you mend a wrong subtraction by doing your addition right.

—AB

Money

There is no escape from sordidness but by being free from money-craving, with all its base hopes and temptations, its watching for death, its hinted requests, its horse-dealer's desire to make bad work pass for good, its seeking for function which ought to be another's, its compulsion often to long for Luck in the shape of a wide calamity.

—MM

There is a pale shade of bribery which is sometimes called prosperity.

—MM

Morality

Our lives make a moral tradition for our individual selves, as the life of mankind at large makes a moral tradition for the race, and to have once acted nobly seems a reason why we should always be noble.

—ROM

To the common run of mankind it has always seemed a proof of mental vigour to find moral questions easy, and judge conduct according to concise alternatives.

—ROM

Every objection can be answered if you take broad ground enough . . . no special question of conduct can be properly settled in that way.

—DD

Consequences are unpitying. Our deeds carry their terrible consequences, quite apart from any fluctuations that went before—consequences that are hardly ever confined to ourselves.

—AB

There is a terrible coercion in our deeds which may first turn the honest man into a deceiver, and then reconcile him to the change; for this reason—that the second wrong presents itself to him in the guise of the only practicable right. . . . Europe adjusts itself to a *fait accompli,* and so does an individual character,—until placid adjustment is disturbed by a convulsive retribution.

—AB

If we only look far enough off for the consequences of our actions, we can always find some point in the combination of results by which those actions can be justified: by adopting the point of view of a Providence who arranges results, or of a philosopher who traces them, we shall find it possible to obtain perfect complacency in choosing to do what is most agreeable to us in the present moment.

—MOF

The same society has had a gibbet for the murderer and a gibbet for the martyr, an execrating hiss for a dastardly act and as loud a hiss for many a word of generous truthfulness or just insight: a mixed condition of things which is the sign, not of hopeless confusion, but of struggling order.

—ROM

The great problem of the shifting relation between passion and duty is clear to no man who is capable of apprehending it. . . . the truth, that moral judgments must remain false and hollow, unless they are checked and enlightened by a perpetual reference to the special circumstances that mark the individual lot.

—MOF

The more deeply we penetrate into the knowledge of society in its details the more thoroughly we shall be convinced that a universal social policy has no validity except on paper.

—WR

So long as a belief in propositions is regarded as indispensable to salvation, the pursuit of truth *as such* is not possible, any more than it is possible for a man who is swimming for his life to make meteorological observations on the storm which threatens to overwhelm him.

—WR

Motherhood

A mother's love, I often say, is like a tree that has got all the wood in it, from the very first it made.

—DD

It is easier to find an old mother than an old friend. Friendships begin with liking or gratitude—roots that can be pulled up. Mother's love begins deeper down.

—DD

Milk and mildness are not the best things for keeping, and when they turn a little sour, they may disagree with young stomachs seriously. I have often wondered whether those early Madonnas of Raphael, with the blond faces and somewhat stupid expression, kept their placidity undisturbed when their strong-limbed, strong-willed boys got a little too old to do without clothing. I think they must have been given to feeble remonstrance, getting more and more peevish as it became more and more ineffectual.

—MOF

Narrow Minds

To minds strongly marked by the positive and negative qualities that create severity—strength of will, conscious rectitude of purpose, narrowness of imagination and intellect, great power of self-control, and a disposition to exert controls over others—prejudices come as the natural food of tendencies which can get no sustenance out of that complex, fragmentary, doubt-provoking knowledge which we call truth.

—MOF

All people of broad, strong sense have an instinctive repugnance to the man of maxims; because such people early discern that the mysterious complexity of our life is not to be embraced by maxims, and that to lace ourselves up in formulas of that sort is to repress all the divine promptings and inspirations that spring from growing insight and sympathy.

—MOF

The man of maxims is the popular representative of the minds that are guided in their moral judgment solely by general rules, thinking that these will lead them to justice by a ready-made patent method, without the trouble of exerting patience, discrimination, impartiality—without any care to assure themselves whether they have the insight that comes from a hardly-earned estimate of temptation, or from a life vivid and intense enough to have created a wide fellow-feeling with all that is human.

—MOF

Obligation
Nature herself occasionally quarters an inconvenient parasite on an animal towards whom she has otherwise no ill-will. What then? We admire her care for the parasite.

—MOF

Open-Mindedness
Receptiveness is a rare and massive power, like fortitude.

—DD

Parties
Hostesses who entertain much must make up their parties as ministers make up their cabinets, on grounds other than personal liking.

—DD

Passion

Our love is inwrought in our enthusiasm as electricity is inwrought in the air, exalting its power by a subtle presence.

—AB

Most of us who turn to any subject we love remember some morning or evening hour when we got on a high stool to reach down an untried volume, or sat with parted lips listening to a new talker, or for very lack of books began to listen to the voices within, as the first traceable beginnings of our love.

—MM

A man may make a good appearance in high social positions—may be supposed to know the classics, to have his reserves on science, a strong though repressed opinion on politics, and all the sentiments of the English gentleman, at a small expense of vital energy.

—DD

We object less to be taxed with the enslaving excess of our passions than with our deficiency in wider passion; but if the truth were known, our reputed intensity is often the dulness of not knowing what else to do with ourselves.

—DD

May not a man silence his awe or his love and take to finding reasons, which others demand? But if his love lies deeper than any reasons to be found? Man finds his pathways.

—DD

If . . . energetic belief, pursuing a grand and remote end, is often in danger of becoming a demon-worship, in which

the votary lets his son and daughter pass through the fire
with a readiness that hardly looks like sacrifice; tender
fellow-feeling for the nearest has its danger too, and is apt
to be timid and sceptical towards the larger aims without
which life cannot rise into religion.

—ROM

The embitterment of hatred is often as unaccountable to on-
lookers as the growth of devoted love, and it not only seems
but is really out of direct relation with any outward causes
to be alleged. Passion is of the nature of seed, and finds
nourishment within, tending to a predominance which determines all currents towards itself, and makes the whole
life its tributary.

—DD

Patience
Fellow-mortals, every one, must be accepted as they are:
you can neither straighten their noses, nor brighten their
wit, not rectify their dispositions; and it is these people—
amongst whom your life is passed—that it is needful you
should tolerate, pity, and love: it is these more or less ugly,
stupid, inconsistent people, whose movements of goodness
you should be able to admire—for whom you should cher-
ish all possible hopes, all possible patience.

—AB

It's easy finding reasons why other folks should be patient.

—AB

Persistence
Mild persistence . . . as we know, enables a white soft living
substance to make its way in spite of opposing rock.

—MM

Perspective

A lap-dog would be necessarily at a loss in framing to itself the motives and adventures of doghood at large.

—DD

What we see exclusively we are apt to see with some mistake of proportions.

—DD

It is to be believed that attendance at the *opera bouffe* in the present day would not leave men's minds entirely without shock, if the manners observed there with some applause were suddenly to start up in their own families. Perspective, as its inventor remarked, is a beautiful thing. What horrors of damp huts, where human beings languish, may not become picturesque through aerial distance!

—DD

Philosophy

The driest argument has its hallucinations, too hastily concluding that its net will now at last be large enough to hold the universe.

—DD

We must be patient with the inevitable makeshift of our human thinking, whether in its sum total or in the separate minds that have made the sum.

—DD

Ideas are a sort of parliament, but there's a commonwealth outside, and a good deal of the commonwealth is working at change without knowing what the parliament is doing.

—DD

Poetry

To be a poet is to have a soul so quick to discern, that no shade of quality escapes it, and so quick to feel, that discernment is but a hand playing with finely-ordered variety on the chords of emotion—a soul in which knowledge passes instantaneously into feeling, and feeling flashes back as a new organ of knowledge. One may have that condition by fits only.

—MM

Politics

Parliament, like the rest of our lives, even to our eating and apparel, could hardly go on if our imaginations were too active about processes.

—MM

There's no action possible without a little acting.

—DD

It is one thing to say, "In this particular case I am forced to put on this foolscap and grin," and another to buy a pocket foolscap and practise myself in grinning.

—DD

I'm not sure that men are the fondest of those who try to be useful to them. . . . You must make it quite clear to your mind which you are most bent upon . . . popularity or usefulness—else you may happen to miss both.

—AB

The cause of freedom . . . is often most injured by the enemies who carry within them the power of certain human virtues. The wickedest man is often not the most insurmountable obstacle to the triumph of good.

—ROM

It is the lot of every man who has to speak for the satisfaction of the crowd, that he must often speak in virtue of yesterday's faith, hoping it will come back tomorrow.

—ROM

To have a mind well oiled with that sort of argument which prevents any claim from grasping it, seems eminently convenient sometimes, only the oil becomes objectionable when we find it anointing other minds on which we want to establish a hold.

—ROM

Potential

There be [those] who hold that the deeper tragedy were a Prometheus Bound not *after* but *before* he has well got the celestial fire . . . thrust by . . . instituted methods into a solitude of despised ideas, fastened in throbbing helplessness by the fatal pressure of poverty and disease—a solitude where many pass by, but none regard.

—DD

Prayer

The most powerful movement of feeling with a liturgy is the prayer which seeks for nothing special, but is a yearning to escape from limitations of our own weakness and an invocation to all Good to enter and abide with us; or else a self-oblivious lifting up of gladness, a *Gloria in excelsis* that such Good exists; both the yearning and the exultation gathering their utmost force from the sense of communion in a form which has expressed them both, for long generations of struggling fellow-men.

—DD

Prejudices

Prejudices, like odorous bodies, have a double existence both solid and subtle—solid as the pyramids, subtle as the twentieth echo of an echo, or as the memory of hyacinths which once scented the darkness.

—MM

Pride

Little achievement is required in order to pity another man's shortcomings.

—MM

If you are not proud of your cellar, there is no thrill of satisfaction in seeing your guest hold up his wine-glass to the light and look judicial. Such joys are reserved for conscious merit.

—MM

[The] state of not-caring, just as much as desire, [requires] its related object—namely, a world of admiring or envying spectators: for if you are fond of looking stonily at smiling persons, the persons must be there and they must smile—a rudimentary truth which is surely forgotten by those who complain of mankind as generally contemptible, since any other aspect of the race must disappoint the voracity of their contempt.

—DD

Procrastination

What should we all do without the calendar, when we want to put off a disagreeable duty? The admirable arrangements of the solar system, by which our time is measured, always supply us with a term before which it is hardly worthwhile to set about anything we are disinclined to.

—MM

Progress
We have got to examine the nature of changes before we have a warrant to call them progress, which word is supposed to include a bettering, though I apprehend it to be ill chosen for that purpose, since mere motion onward may carry us to a bog or a precipice.

—DD

Prophecy
Among all forms of mistake, prophecy is the most gratuitous.

—MM

Questioning
To *fear* the examination of any proposition appears to me an intellectual and moral palsy that will ever hinder the firm grasping of any substance whatever.

—Correspondence

Racial Stereotyping
It appears the Caribs, who know little of theology, regard thieving as a practice peculiarly connected with Christian tenets, and probably they could allege experimental grounds for this opinion.

—DD

Rash Judgments
For getting a strong impression that a skein is tangled, there is nothing like snatching hastily at a single thread.

—MOF

A disagreeable resolve formed in the chill hours of the morning [has] as many conditions against it as the early frost, and rarely [persists] under the warming influences of the day.

—MM

Reality

Here undoubtedly lies the chief poetic energy: in the force of imagination that pierces or exalts the solid fact, instead of floating among cloud-pictures.

—DD

The fervour of sympathy with which we contemplate a grandiose martyrdom is feeble compared with the enthusiasm that keeps unslacked where there is no danger, no challenge—nothing but impartial midday falling on commonplace.

—DD

That hard unaccommodating Actual . . . has never consulted our taste and is entirely unselect. Enthusiasm, we know, dwells at ease among ideas, tolerates garlic breathed in the middle-ages, and sees no shabbiness in the official trappings of classic processions: it gets squeamish when ideals press upon it as something warmly incarnate, and can hardly face them without fainting.

—DD

Those slight indirect suggestions which are dependent on apparently trivial coincidences and incalculable states of mind, are the favourite machinery of Fact, but are not the stuff in which imagination is apt to work.

—MOF

We want to be taught to feel, not for the heroic artisan or the sentimental peasant, but for the peasant in all his coarse apathy, and the artisan in all his suspicious selfishness.

—WR

All the more sacred is the task of the artist when he undertakes to paint the life of the People. It is not so very serious that we should have false ideas about evanescent fashions—about the manners and conversations of beaux and duchesses; but it *is* serious that our sympathy with the perennial joys and struggles, the toil, the tragedy, and the humor in the life of our more heavily-laden fellow-men, should be perverted, and turned towards a false object instead of the true one.

—Essays

Realism—the doctrine that all truth and beauty are to be attained by a humble and faithful study of nature, and not by substituting vague forms, bred by imagination on the mists of feeling, in place of definite, substantial reality.

—WR

Reflection
That agreeable after-glow of excitement when thought lapses from examination of a specific object into a suffusive sense of its connections with all the rest of our existence— seems, as it were, to throw itself on its back after vigorous swimming and float with the repose of unexhausted strength.

—MM

Reform
Reformation, where a man can afford to do without it, can hardly be other than genuine.

—DD

Relationships
Loneliness is more lonely than distrust.

—MM

Religion

The best piety is to enjoy—when you can. You are doing the most then to save the earth's character as an agreeable planet. And enjoyment radiates.

—MM

There is no general doctrine which is not capable of eating out our morality if unchecked by the deep-seated habit of direct fellow-feeling with individual fellow men.

—MM

Religion can only change when the emotions which fill it are changed; and the religion of personal fear remains nearly at the level of the savage.

—MM

Terror of the unseen is so far above mere sensual cowardice that it will annihilate that cowardice: it is the initial recognition of a moral law restraining desire, and checks the hard bold scrutiny of imperfect thought into obligations. . . . "It is good," sing the old Eumenides in Aeschylus, "that fear should sit as the guardian of the soul, forcing it into wisdom". . . . That guardianship may become needless; but only. . . when duty and love have united in one stream and made a common force.

—ROM

If I have read religious history aright—faith, hope, and charity have not always been found in a direct ratio with sensibility to the three concords; and it is possible . . . to have very erroneous theories and very sublime feelings.

—AB

A modern simpleton who swallowed whole one of the old systems of philosophy, and took the indigestion it occasioned for the signs of a divine afflux or the voice of an inward monitor, might see his interest in a form of self-conceit which he called self-rewarding virtue.

—ROM

The soul gets more hungry when the body is ill at ease.

—AB

Doctrines [are] like finding names for your feelings, so . . . you can talk of 'em when you've never known 'em.

—AB

Life, though a good to men on the whole, is a doubtful good to many, and to some not a good at all. To my thought, it is a source of constant mental distortion to make the denial of this a part of religion, to go on pretending things are better than they are.

—Correspondence

There [are] human beings who never saw angels or heard perfectly clear messages. Such truth as came to them was brought confusedly in the voices and deeds of men not at all like the seraphs of unfailing wing and piercing vision . . . these beings unvisited by angels had no other choice than to grasp the stumbling guidance along the path of reliance and action which is the path of life, or else to pause in loneliness and disbelief, which is no path, but the arrest of inaction and death.

—ROM

Human love and pity are a ground of faith in some other love.

—AB

Reputation
Who can know how much of his most inward life is made
up of the thoughts he believes other men to have about him,
until that fabric of opinion is threatened with ruin?

—MM

Revenge
Prosperous men take a little vengeance now and then, as
they take a diversion, when it comes easily in their way, and
is no hindrance to business; and such small unimpassioned
revenges have an enormous effect in life, running through
all degrees of pleasant infliction, blocking the fit men out of
places, and blackening characters in unpremeditated talk.
Still more, to see people who have been only insignificantly
offensive to us, reduced in life and humiliated without any
special effort of ours, is apt to have a soothing, flattering influence: Providence, or some other prince of this world, it
appears, has undertaken the task of retribution for us; and
really, by an agreeable constitution of things, our enemies
somehow *don't* prosper.

—MOF

Revolution
It is one thing to like defiance, and another thing to like its
consequences.

—MM

We may handle even extreme opinions with impunity while
our furniture, our dinner-giving, and preference for armor-
ial bearings in our own case, link us indissolubly with the
established order.

—MM

Here is a restraint which nature and society have provided
on the pursuit of striking adventure; so that a soul burning

with a sense of what the universe is not, and ready to take all existence as fuel, is nevertheless held captive by the ordinary wire-work of social forms and does nothing in particular.

—DD

Romantic Ideas

Perhaps poetry and romance are as plentiful as ever in the world except for those phlegmatic natures who I suspect would in any age have regarded them as a dull form of erroneous thinking. They exist very easily in the same room with the microscope and even in railway carriages: what banishes them is the vacuum in gentlemen and lady passengers.

—DD

Roots

The best introduction to astronomy is to think of the nightly heavens as a little lot of stars belonging to one's own homestead.

—DD

There is no sense of ease like the ease we felt in those scenes where we were born, where objects became dear to us before we had known the labour of choice, and where the outer world seemed only an extension of our personality.

—MOF

A human life, I think, should be well-rooted in some spot of native land . . . for whatever will give that early home a familiar unmistakable difference amidst the future of knowledge: a spot where the definiteness of early memories may be inwrought with affection and kindly acquaintance with all neighbors, even to the dogs and donkeys, may spread not by sentimental effort and reflection, but as a sweet habit of the blood.

—DD

We could never have loved the earth so well if we had had no childhood in it—if it were not the earth where the same flowers come up again every spring that we used to gather with our tiny fingers. . . . What novelty is worth that sweet monotony where everything is known, and *loved* because it is known? . . . such things as these are the mother tongue of our imagination, the language that is laden with all the subtle inextricable associations the fleeting hours of our childhood left behind them.

—MOF

There are some plants that have hardly any roots: you may tear them from their native nook of rock or wall, and just lay them over your ornamental flower-pot, and they blossom none the worse.

—AB

Sacrifice
Was there ever a young lady or gentleman not ready to give up an unspecified indulgence for the sake of the favourite one specified?

—DD

Saying Good-bye, Again
It is certainly trying to a man's dignity to reappear when he is not expected to do so: a first farewell has pathos in it, but to come back for a second lends an opening to comedy.

—MM

Science

Science is properly more scrupulous than dogma. Dogma gives charter to mistake, but the very breath of science is a contest with mistake, and must keep the conscience alive.

—MM

Even strictly-measuring science could hardly have got on without that forecasting ardour which feels the agitations of discovery beforehand, and has a faith in its preconception that surmounts many failures of experiment. And in relation to human motives and actions, passionate belief has a fuller efficacy.

—DD

Scruples

Notions and scruples [are] like spilt needles, making one afraid of treading or sitting down, or even eating.

—MM

Security

The sense of security more frequently springs from habit than from conviction, and for this reason it often subsists after such a change in the conditions as might have been expected to suggest alarm. The lapse of time during which a given event has not happened, is, in this logic of habit, constantly alleged as a reason why the event should never happen, even when the lapse of time is precisely the added condition which makes the event imminent.

—SM

Self-Fulfillment

Full souls are double mirrors, making still an endless vista of fair things before, repeating things behind.

—MM

Self-Sacrifice
Love has a habit of saying "Never mind" to angry self, who, sitting down for the nonce in the lower place, by-and-by gets used to it.

—DD

Selfishness
Selfish [is] a judgment readily passed by those who have never tested their own power of sacrifice.

—SM

Sensitivity
Heat is a great agent and a useful word, but considered as a means of explaining the universe it requires an extensive knowledge of differences; and as a means of explaining character 'sensitiveness' is in much the same predicament.

—DD

To . . . keep sentiment alive and active, [is] something like the famous recipe for making cannon—to first take a round hole and then enclose it with iron.

—DD

Seriousness
I can't wear my solemnity too often, else it will go to rags.

—MM

Setbacks
There are certain animals to which tenacity of position is a law of life—they can never flourish again, after a single wrench: and there are certain human beings to whom predominance is a law of life—they can only sustain humiliation so long as they can refuse to believe in it, and, in their own conception, predominate still.

—MOF

Short-Sightedness

In the vain laughter of folly wisdom hears half its applause.

—ROM

Snobs

A man who seems to have been able to command the best, has a sovereign power of depreciation.

—DD

Social Pressures

There is no creature whose inward being is so strong that it is not greatly determined by what lies outside it.

—MM

Social Skills

Good society floated on gossamer wings of light irony, is of very expensive production.

—MOF

We are more distinctly conscious that rude penances are out of the question for gentlemen in an enlightened age, and that mortal sin is not incompatible with an appetite for muffins; an assault on our pockets, which in more barbarous times would have been made in the brusque form of a pistol-shot, is quite a well-bred and smiling procedure now it has become a request for a loan thrown in an easy parenthesis between the second and third glasses of claret.

—AB

Sorrow

There is much pain that is quite noiseless; and vibrations that make human agonies are often a mere whisper in the roar of hurrying existence.

—FH

That element of tragedy which lies in the very fact of frequency, has not yet wrought itself into the coarse emotion of mankind; and perhaps our frames could hardly bear much of it. If we had a keen vision and feeling of all ordinary human life, it would be like hearing the grass grow and the squirrel's heart beat, and we should die of that roar which lies on the other side of silence. As it is, the quickest of us walk about well wadded with stupidity.

—MM

For there is no hour that has not its births of gladness and despair, no morning brightness that does not bring new sickness to desolation as well as new forces to genius and love. . . . We are children of a large family, and must learn, as such children do, not to expect that our little hurts will be made much of—to be content with little nurture and caressing, and help each other the more.

—AB

Surely if we could recall that early bitterness, and the dim guesses, the strangely perspectiveless conception of life that gave the bitterness its intensity, we should not pooh-pooh the griefs of our children.

—MOF

The Soul
Let thy chief terror be thine own soul.

—DD

1st Gent. An ancient land in ancient oracles
Is called "law thirsty": all the struggle there
Was after order and perfect rule.
Pray, where lie such lands now? . . .
2nd Gent. Why, where they lay of old—in human souls.

—MM

The Stock Market

The degrees of liberty a man allows himself with other people's property being often delicately drawn, even beyond the boundary where the law begins to lay its hold . . . is the reason why spoons are a safer investment than mining shares.

—DD

Strangers

One can begin so many things with a new person!—even begin to be a better man.

—MM

Stubbornness

There is a sort of human paste that when it comes near the fire of enthusiasm is only baked into a harder shape.

—DD

Success

Cheerful, successful worldliness has a false air of being more selfish than the acrid, unsuccessful kind, whose secret history is summed up in the terrible words, "Sold but not paid for."

—DD

Symbolism

Signs are small measurable things, but interpretations are illimitable.

—MM

Sympathy

More helpful than all wisdom is one draught of simple human pity that will not forsake us.

—MOF

Thinking

We mortals have a strange spiritual chemistry going on within us, so that a lazy stagnation or even a cottony milkiness may be preparing one knows not what biting or explosive material.

—DD

Time

No story is the same to us after a lapse of time, or rather, we who read it are no longer the same interpreters.

—AB

All ripeness beneath the sun has a further stage, less esteemed in the market.

—MOF

Tolerance

The responsibility of tolerance lies with those who have the wider vision.

WIDEN   VISION   —MOF

Tradition

Kind Providence furnishes the limpest personality with a little gum or starch in the form of tradition.

—MM

Tragedy

The pride and obstinacy of millers, and other insignificant people, whom you pass unnoticingly on the road everyday, have their tragedy too; but it is of that unwept, hidden sort, that goes on from generation to generation, and leaves no record.

—MOF

Trust

No soul is desolate as long as there is a human being for whom it can feel trust and reverence.

—ROM

Those who trust us educate us.

—DD

Truth

There seems to be no reason why a loud man should not be given to concealment of anything except his own voice, unless it can be shown that Holy Writ has placed the seat of candour in the lungs.

—MM

Wrong reasoning sometimes lands poor mortals in the right conclusions: starting a long way off the true point, and proceeding by loops and zigzags, we now and then arrive just where we ought to be.

—MM

Our naked feelings make haste to clothe themselves in propositions which lie at hand among our store of opinions . . . to give a true account of what passes within us something else is necessary besides sincerity.

—ROM

Uncelebrated Lives

For the growing good of the world is partly dependent on unhistoric acts; and that things are not so ill with you and me as they might have been, is half owing to the number who lived faithfully a hidden life, and rest in unvisited tombs.

—MM

Vanity
The desire to know that one has not looked an absolute fright during a few hours of conversation, may be construed as lying within the bonds of a laudable benevolent consideration for others.

—MOF

Vision
"Second-sight" is a flag over disputed ground.

—DD

To glory in a prophetic vision of knowledge covering the earth, is an easier exercise of believing imagination than to see its beginning in newspaper placards, staring at you from a bridge beyond the corn-fields; and it might well happen to most of us dainty people that we were in the thick of the battle of Armageddon without being aware of anything more than the annoyance of a little explosive smoke and struggling on the ground immediately about us.

—DD

No doubt there are abject specimens of the visionary, as there is a minim mammal which you might imprison in the finger of your glove. That small relative of the elephant has no harm in him; but what great mental or social type is free from specimens whose insignificance is both ugly and noxious? One is afraid to think of all that the genus "patriot" embraces; or of the elbowing there might be at the day of judgment for those who ranked as authors, and brought volumes either in their hands or on trucks.

—DD

Since the unemotional intellect may carry us into a mathematical dreamland where nothing is but what is not, per-

haps an emotional intellect may have absorbed into its passionate vision of possibilities some truth of what will be.

—DD

Columbus had some impressions about himself which we
call superstitions and used some arguments which we dis-
approve; but he had also some true physical conceptions,
and he had the passionate patience of genius to make them
tell on mankind. The world has made up its mind rather
contemptuously about those who were deaf to Columbus.

—DD

War

It is doubtful whether our soldiers would be maintained if
there were not pacific people at home who like to fancy
themselves soldiers. War, like other dramatic spectacles,
might possibly cease for want of a "public."

—MOF

Withholding Love

It is in these acts called trivialities that the seeds of joy are
for ever wasted, until men and women look round with
haggard faces at the devastation their own waste has made,
and say, the earth bears no harvest of sweetness—calling
their denial knowledge.

—MM

Women

I'm not denyin' the women are foolish: God Almighty made
'em to match the men.

—AB

We are apt to be kinder to the brutes that love us than to the
women that love us. Is it because the brutes are dumb?

—AB

So it has been since the days of Hecuba and of Hector, Tamer of horses: inside the gates the women with streaming hair and uplifted hands offering prayers, watching the world's combat from afar, filling their long, empty days with memories and fears: outside, the men, in fierce struggle with things divine and human, quenching memory in the stronger light of purpose, losing the sense of dread and even of wounds in the hurrying ardour of action.

—MOF

We women can't go in search of adventures—to find out the North-West Passage or the source of the Nile, or to hunt tigers in the East. We must stay where we grow, or where the gardeners like to transplant us. We are brought up like the flowers, to look as pretty as we can, and be dull without complaining. That is my notion about the plants: they are often bored, and that is the reason why some of them have got poisonous.

—DD

In that curious compound, the feminine character, it may easily happen that the flavour is unpleasant in spite of excellent ingredients.

—MOF

[I find] just that kernel of truth in the vulgar alarm of men lest women should be "unsexed," arguing that we cannot afford to part with that exquisite type of gentleness, tenderness, possibly maternity, suffusing a woman's being with affectionateness, which makes what we mean by the feminine character.

—Correspondence

Women are specially framed for the love which feels possession in renouncing.

—DD

Excessive rumination and self-questioning is perhaps a morbid habit inevitable to a mind of much moral sensibility when shut out from its due share of outward activity and of practical claims on its affections—inevitable to a noble-hearted, childless women, when her lot is narrow. "I can do so little—have I done it all well?" is the perpetually recurring thought; and there are no voices calling her away from that soliloquy, no preemptory demands to divert energy from vain regret or superfluous scruple.

—SM

It is a fact perhaps kept a little too much in the background, that mothers have a self larger than their maternity and that when their sons have come to be taller than themselves and are gone from college off into the world, there are wide spaces of time which are not filled with praying for their boys, reading old letters and envying yet blessing those who are attending to their shirt buttons.

—FH

A man is seldom ashamed of feeling that he cannot love a woman so well when he sees a certain greatness in her: nature having intended greatness for men.

—MM

By a peculiar thermometric adjustment, when a woman's talent is at zero, journalistic approbation is at the boiling pitch; when she attains mediocrity, it is already at no more than summer heat; and if ever she reaches excellence, critical enthusiasm drops to the freezing point.

—WR

Work
Every man's work, pursued steadily, tends in this way to become an end in itself, and so to bridge over the loveless chasms of his life.

—SM

Are there many situations more sublimely tragic than the struggle of the soul with the demand to renounce a work which as been all the significance of its life—a significance which is to vanish as the waters which come and go where no man has need of them?

—MM

In general mortals have a great power of being astonished at the presence of an effect towards which they have done everything, and at the absence of an effect towards which they have done nothing but desire it.

—DD

Wrinkles
The days and the months pace over us like restless little birds, and leave the marks of their feet backwards and forwards; especially when they are like birds with heavy hearts—then they tread heavily.

—DD

Writing
I am content to tell my simple story without trying to make things seem better than they were; dreading nothing, indeed, but falsity, which in spite of one's best efforts, there is reason to dread.

—AB

[I aspire] to give no more than a faithful account of men and things as they have mirrored themselves in my mind. The mirror is doubtless defective, the outlines will sometimes be disturbed; the reflection faint or confused; but I feel as much bound to tell you, as precisely as I can, what that reflection is, as if I were on the witness box narrating my experience on oath.

—AB

Who shall tell what may be the effect of writing? If it happens to have been cut in stone, though it lie face downmost for ages on a forsaken beach, or "rest quietly under the drums and tramplings of many conquests" . . . it may end by letting us into the secret of usurpations and other scandals gossiped about long empires ago: this world being apparently a huge whispering-gallery. Such conditions are often minutely represented in our petty lifetime.

—MM

It was doubtless an ingenious idea to call the camel the ship of the desert, but it would hardly lead one far in training that useful beast. O Aristotle! if you had the advantage of being "the freshest modern" instead of the greatest ancient, would you not have mingled your praise of metaphorical speech, as a sign of high intelligence, with a lamentation that intelligence so rarely shows itself in speech without metaphor—that we can so seldom declare what a thing is, except by saying it is something else?

—MOF

If art does not enlarge men's sympathies, it does nothing morally. I have had heart-cutting experience that *opinions* are a poor cement between human souls.

—Correspondence

[A novelist] does not make [knowledge] a pedestal from which she flatters herself that she commands a complete view of men and things, but makes it a point of observation from which to form a right estimate of herself.

—WR

The fantastic or the boldly imaginative poet may be as sincere as the most realistic: he is true to his own sensibilities or inward vision, and in his wildest flights he never breaks loose from his criterion—the truth of his own mental state.

—WR

Does not science tell us that its highest striving is after the ascertainment of a unity which shall bind the smallest things with the greatest? In natural science, I have understood, there is nothing petty to the mind that has a large vision of relations, and to which every single object suggests a vast sum of conditions. It is surely the same with the observation of human life.

—MOF

[Never] lapse from the picture to the diagram.

—Correspondence

Youth
The first impulse of a young and ingenuous mind is to withhold the slightest sanction from all that contains even a mixture of supposed error. When the soul is just liberated from the wretched giant's bed of dogmas on which it has been racked and stretched ever since it began to think there is a feeling of exultation and strong hope.

—Written to her friend Sara Hennell when
Mary Ann Evans was 23 years old

A vigorous young mind not overbalanced by passion, finds a good in making acquaintance with life, and watches its own powers with interest.

—MM

The difficult task of knowing another soul is not for young
gentlemen whose consciousness is chiefly made up of their
own wishes.

—MM

It is as hard to a boy or girl to believe that a great wretched-
ness will actually befall them, as to believe that they will
die.

—AB

These bitter sorrows of childhood! when sorrow is all new
and strange, when hope has not yet got wings to fly beyond
the days and weeks, and the space from summer to summer seems measureless.

—MOF

That first crisis of a passionate youthful rebellion against
what is not fitly called pain, but rather the absence of joy—
that first rage of disappointment in life's morning, which
we whom the years have subdued are apt to remember but
dimly as part of our own experience and so to be intolerant
of its self-enclosed unreasonableness and impiety. What
passion seems more absurd, when we have got outside it
and looked at calamity as a collective risk, than this amazed
anguish.

—DD

It is very weak-minded to make your creed up by the rule
of contrary. Still one may honour one's parents, without following their notions exactly, any more than the exact cut of
their clothing.

—DD

Young reverence for one who is also young is the most coer-
cive of all: there is the same level of temptation, and the

higher motive is believed in as a fuller force—not suspected to be a mere residue from weary experience.

—DD

Secrets leave no lines in young faces.

—AB

SUGGESTED READING BY AND
ABOUT GEORGE ELIOT

The Major Novels
Scenes of Clerical Life (1858)
Adam Bede (1859)
Mill on the Floss (1860)
Silas Marner (1861)
Romola (1863)
Felix Holt, The Radical (1866)
Middlemarch (1872)
Daniel Deronda (1876)

Additional Reading

Ashton, Rosemary: *George Eliot*. New York and Oxford: Oxford University Press, 1983.

Byatt, A. S., and Nicholas Warren, eds. *George Eliot: Selected Essays, Poems and Other Writings*. Harmondsworth: Penguin, 1990.

Bodenheimer, Rosemarie. *The Real Life of Mary Ann Evans: George Eliot, Her Letters and Fiction*. Ithaca: Cornell University Press, 1994.

Haight, Gordon S. *George Eliot: A Biography*. New York and Oxford: Oxford University Press, 1968.

Haight, Gordon S., ed. *The George Eliot Letters, 9 vols.* New Haven: Yale University Press, 1954–78.

Harris, Margaret, and Judith Johnston, eds. *The Journals of George Eliot.* Cambridge: Cambridge University Press, 1998.

Hughes, Kathryn. *George Eliot: The Last Victorian.* New York: Farrar, Straus & Giroux, 1998.

Levine, George, ed. *The Cambridge Campanion to George Eliot.* Cambridge: Cambridge University Press, 2001.

Pinney, Thomas, ed. *Essays of George Eliot.* New York: Columbia University Press, 1963.

Mill on the Floss

Silas Marner

Adam Bede

Daniel Deronda

Middlemarch

novels..., experiments
in life"
works ... confront the
same dilemmas ...
we struggle with
today